GEORGIA STATE BUCKET JOURNAL

Visit the State Parks of Georgia, USA

This book belongs to

_____

If found please call

_____

"**This was wild country** when Muir passed through here in 1867. The Cherokees had only been removed a few decades earlier and Muir described it as "the most primitive country I have ever seen, primitive in everything." ~Brent Martin

"**Talking about oh Georgia** take me to your Southlands, I sometimes feel that life is rolling on, Oh Georgia lead me through your heartlands, I need to see them one more time before they're gone. ~Elton John

"**Two great rivers** rise in the northeast: the Savannah, which forms part of the border with South Carolina, and the Chattahoochee, which flows across the state to become the western boundary."

GEORGIA STATE PARKS BUCKET JOURNAL

©2020 by My Bucket Journals LLC
Hutto, Texas 78634

Designed and printed in the USA. All rights reserved.

This publication may not be reproduced stored or transmitted in whole or in part, in any form or by any means, electronic, mechanical or otherwise, without prior written consent from the publisher and author.

Brief quotations may be included in a review. If in PDF form, it may be stored on your computer and you may keep one online digital copy. This publication may be printed for personal use only.

Disclaimer
The information in this book is based on the author's opinion, knowledge and experience. The publisher and the author will not be held liable for the use or misuse of the information contained herein.

Disclosure
This book may contain affiliate links. If you click through an affiliate link to a third-party website and make a purchase, the author may receive a small commission.

Cover photo ©DepositPhotos

The State of Georgia is a tumbling landscape, starting with the Blue Ridge Mountains sloping to the piedmont region turning into the coastal plain. With more than 35 lakes and an extensive shoreline, Georgia offers many outdoor adventures.

Some of the parks in the journal are well known and some are less traveled, all are waiting for you to discover their unique qualities.

In this Georgia State Parks & Historic Sites Bucket Journal, **you will find individual pages for 72 state parks** in the beautiful State of Georgia. Many allow for overnight camping and all are great for day use trips.

This bucket journal is different. It gives you the ability to create your own unique exploration of whichever state park or historic site you choose

How to Use Your Georgia State Parks Bucket Journal

Parks that offer camping or other accommodations are on orange pages.
- Search out details about the state park or recreational site by using the website URL provided.
- Have fun planning the things you want to see on the left side of the 2-page spread.
- This is best done before you take your trip, but can be done while you are out exploring.
- On the right side, chronicle everything that you do and experience. Included is space for journaling and reflection about your stay in the park.

Parks that are Day Use Area Only are on yellow pages.
- Day use parks are still fun to visit, even if you can't sleep there.
- Visit them when you are staying at other overnight parks or use them as day trip excursions to get out and explore.

The Georgia State Parks & Historic Sites Bucket Journal will become a living memory for your trips and adventures as you discover the wonders of the state.

Enjoy exploring the beauty and history that is Georgia!

TABLE OF CONTENTS

- ☐ State Map..................................6

North Georgia Mountains Region Parks........................7
Overnight Parks
- ☐ Red Top Mountain State Park..........8
- ☐ James H. Floyd State Park..............10
- ☐ Cloudland Canyon State Park........12
- ☐ Amicalola Falls State Park & Lodge..................................14
- ☐ Rocky Mountain Recreation & PFA..................................16
- ☐ Fort Mountain State Park...............18
- ☐ Moccasin Creek State Park............20
- ☐ Black Rock Mountain SP.................22
- ☐ Tallulah Gorge State Park...............24
- ☐ Vogel State Park............................26
- ☐ Smithgall Woods State Park...........28
- ☐ Unicoi State Park & Lodge..............30

Day Use Parks
- ☐ Etowah Indian Mounds SHS...........32
- ☐ New Echota State Historic Site......33
- ☐ Resaca Battlefield...........................34
- ☐ Dahlonega Gold Museum SHS.......35
- ☐ Chief Vann House State HS............36
- ☐ Pickett's Mill Battlefield SHS..........37
- ☐ Hardman Farm State HS.................38

Piedmont Region Parks.........39
Overnight Parks
- ☐ Fort Yargo State Park......................40
- ☐ Indian Springs State Park...............42
- ☐ Mistletoe State Park.......................44
- ☐ Chattahoochee Bend State Park...46
- ☐ Sweetwater Creek State Park........48
- ☐ Richard B. Russell State Park.........50
- ☐ Tugaloo State Park.........................52
- ☐ Victoria Bryant State Park..............54

Piedmont Region Parks cont.
Overnight Parks
- ☐ Don Carter State Park.....................56
- ☐ F. D. Roosevelt State Park...............58
- ☐ Hartwell Lakeside Park 60
- ☐ Panola Mountain State Park..........62
- ☐ Elijah Clark State Park....................64
- ☐ Watson Mill Bridge State Park.......66
- ☐ Roosevelt's Little White House State Historic Site..............................68
- ☐ High Falls State Park......................70
- ☐ Hard Labor Creek State Park..........72
- ☐ A.H. Stephens State Park................74
- ☐ Hamburg State Park.......................76

Day Use Parks
- ☐ Jarrell Plantation State HS..............78
- ☐ Traveler's Rest State HS..................79
- ☐ Robert Toombs House State HS.....80

Coastal Plains Region Parks.....................................81
Overnight Parks
- ☐ George T. Bagby State Park............82
- ☐ General Coffee State Park..............84
- ☐ Reed Bingham State Park..............86
- ☐ Georgia Veterans State Park..........88
- ☐ Kolomoki Mounds State Park........90
- ☐ George L. Smith State Park............92
- ☐ Magnolia Springs State Park..........94
- ☐ Seminole State Park......................96
- ☐ Providence Canyon State Outdoor Recreation Area..............................98
- ☐ Florence Marina State Park.........100
- ☐ Jack Hill State Park.......................102
- ☐ Little Ocmulgee State Park & Lodge..................................104

TABLE OF CONTENTS

Coastal Plains Region Parks cont.

Day Use Parks
- ☐ Historic SAM Shortline Railroad..........106
- ☐ Jefferson Davis Memorial SHS.....107
- ☐ Lapham-Patterson House SHS.....108
- ☐ Ball's Ferry Property..........109

Coastal Region Parks..........111

Overnight Parks
- ☐ Laura S. Walker State Park..........112
- ☐ Fort McAllister State Park..........114
- ☐ Crooked River State Park..........116
- ☐ Stephen C. Foster State Park.......118
- ☐ Skidaway Island State Park..........120

Day Use Parks
- ☐ Georgia State Railroad Museum..........122
- ☐ Harper Fowlkes House..........123
- ☐ Old Fort Jackson..........124
- ☐ Pin Point Heritage Museum........125
- ☐ Savannah History Museum..........126
- ☐ Wormsloe State Historic Site......127
- ☐ Hofwyl-Broadfield Plantation State Historic Site..........128
- ☐ Fort Morris State Historic Site....129
- ☐ Fort King George SHS..........130
- ☐ Reynolds Mansion on Sapelo Island..........131

Add More Overnight Parks
- ☐ _____132
- ☐ _____134
- ☐ _____136
- ☐ _____138
- ☐ _____140

Add More Day Use Parks
- ☐ _____142
- ☐ _____143
- ☐ _____144
- ☐ _____145
- ☐ _____146

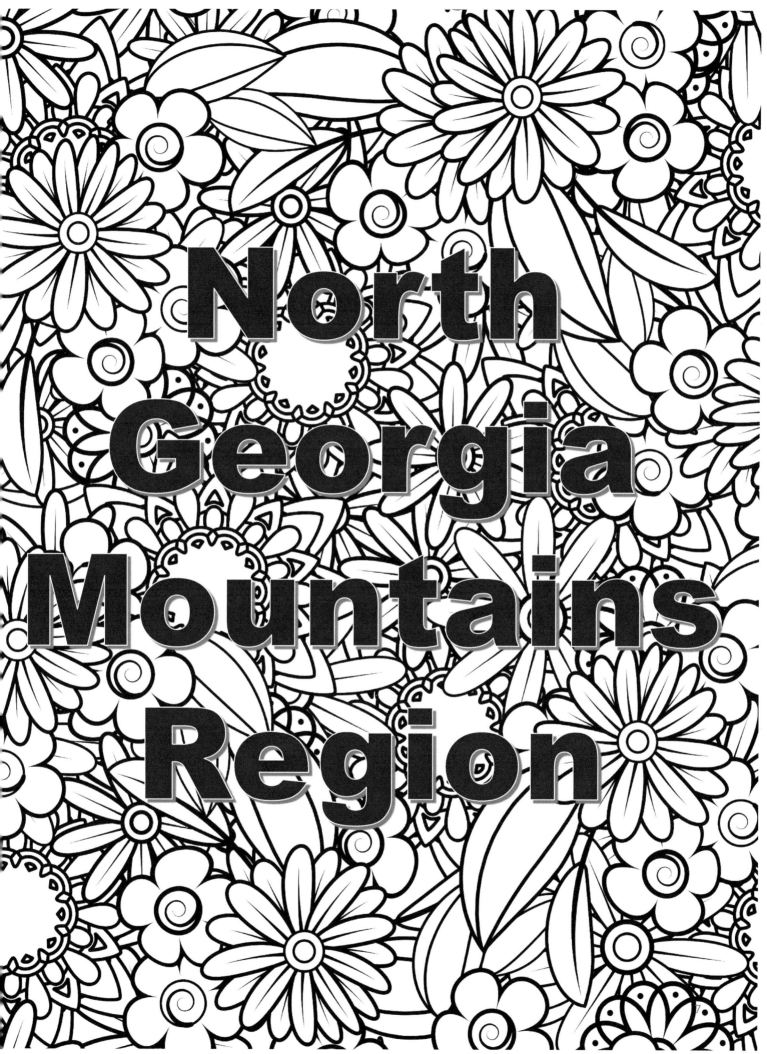

Red Top Mountain State Park
City: Acworth   County: Bartow

Plan your trip: https://gastateparks.org/RedTopMountain

Activities:

- ❏ Archery
- ❏ Biking Trails
- ❏ Boating
- ❏ Canoeing
- ❏ Canyon Climbing
- ❏ Caving
- ❏ Fishing
- ❏ Geocaching
- ❏ Hiking
- ❏ Historic Sites
- ❏ Horseback
- ❏ Hunting
- ❏ Kayaking
- ❏ Nature Programs
- ❏ Photography
- ❏ Rock Climbing
- ❏ Stargazing
- ❏ Swimming
- ❏ Water Skiing
- ❏ Wildlife & Bird Watching
- ❏ Ziplining

Facilities:

- ❏ ADA
- ❏ Picnic sites
- ❏ Restrooms
- ❏ Showers
- ❏ Trailer Access
- ❏ Visitor center
- ❏ Group Camping
- ❏ RV Camp
- ❏ Rustic Camping
- ❏ Cabins / Yurts
- ❏ Day Use Area

Notes:

Get the Facts

- ❏ Phone   770-975-0055
- ❏ Park Hours _____
- ❏ Reservations? ____Y ____N date made_____
- ❏ Open all year ____Y ____N dates_____
- ❏ Check in time _____
- ❏ Check out time _____
- ❏ Pet friendly ____Y ____N
- ❏ Max RV length _____
- ❏ Distance from home
  miles: _____
  hours: _____
- ❏ Address_____

Fees:

- ❏ Day Use $ _____
- ❏ Camp Sites $ _____
- ❏ RV Sites $ _____
- ❏ Refund policy _____

Make It Personal

Trip dates: _____ | The weather was: Sunny Cloudy Rainy Stormy Snowy Foggy Warm Cold

Why I went: _____
_____

How I got there: (circle all that apply)   Plane   Train   Car   Bus   Bike   Hike   RV   MC
_____

I went with: _____

We stayed in (space, cabin # etc): _____

Most relaxing day: _____
_____

Something funny: _____
_____

Someone we met: _____
_____

Best story told: _____
_____

The kids liked this: _____
_____

The best food: _____
_____

Games played: _____
_____

Something disappointing: _____
_____

Next time I'll do this differently: _____
_____

James H. Floyd State Park
City: Summerville   County: Chattooga

Plan your trip: https://gastateparks.org/JamesHFloyd

Activities:

- ❏ Archery
- ❏ Biking Trails
- ❏ Boating
- ❏ Canoeing
- ❏ Canyon Climbing
- ❏ Caving
- ❏ Fishing
- ❏ Geocaching
- ❏ Hiking
- ❏ Historic Sites
- ❏ Horseback
- ❏ Hunting
- ❏ Kayaking
- ❏ Nature Programs
- ❏ Photography
- ❏ Rock Climbing
- ❏ Stargazing
- ❏ Swimming
- ❏ Water Skiing
- ❏ Wildlife & Bird Watching
- ❏ Ziplining

Facilities:

- ❏ ADA
- ❏ Picnic sites
- ❏ Restrooms
- ❏ Showers
- ❏ Trailer Access
- ❏ Visitor center
- ❏ Group Camping
- ❏ RV Camp
- ❏ Rustic Camping
- ❏ Cabins / Yurts
- ❏ Day Use Area

Notes:

Get the Facts

- ❏ Phone 706-857-0826
- ❏ Park Hours _____
- ❏ Reservations? ____Y ____N date made_____
- ❏ Open all year ____Y ____N dates_____
- ❏ Check in time _____
- ❏ Check out time _____
- ❏ Pet friendly ____Y ____N
- ❏ Max RV length _____
- ❏ Distance from home
  miles: _____
  hours: _____
- ❏ Address _____

Fees:

- ❏ Day Use $ _____
- ❏ Camp Sites $ _____
- ❏ RV Sites $ _____
- ❏ Refund policy _____

Make It Personal

Trip dates: _____ | The weather was: Sunny   Cloudy   Rainy   Stormy   Snowy   Foggy   Warm   Cold

Why I went: _____
_____

How I got there: (circle all that apply)   Plane   Train   Car   Bus   Bike   Hike   RV   MC

I went with: _____

We stayed in (space, cabin # etc): _____

Most relaxing day: _____
_____

Something funny: _____
_____

Someone we met: _____
_____

Best story told: _____
_____

The kids liked this: _____
_____

The best food: _____
_____

Games played: _____
_____

Something disappointing: _____
_____

Next time I'll do this differently: _____
_____

Cloudland Canyon State Park
City: Rising Fawn   County: Dade

Plan your trip: https://gastateparks.org/CloudlandCanyon

Activities:

- ❑ Archery
- ❑ Biking Trails
- ❑ Boating
- ❑ Canoeing
- ❑ Canyon Climbing
- ❑ Caving
- ❑ Fishing
- ❑ Geocaching
- ❑ Hiking
- ❑ Historic Sites
- ❑ Horseback
- ❑ Hunting
- ❑ Kayaking
- ❑ Nature Programs
- ❑ Photography
- ❑ Rock Climbing
- ❑ Stargazing
- ❑ Swimming
- ❑ Water Skiing
- ❑ Wildlife & Bird Watching
- ❑ Ziplining
- ❑
- ❑
- ❑
- ❑
- ❑
- ❑
- ❑
- ❑
- ❑
- ❑
- ❑

Facilities:

- ❑ ADA
- ❑ Picnic sites
- ❑ Restrooms
- ❑ Showers
- ❑ Trailer Access
- ❑ Visitor center
- ❑ Group Camping
- ❑ RV Camp
- ❑ Rustic Camping
- ❑ Cabins / Yurts
- ❑ Day Use Area

Notes:

Get the Facts

- ❑ Phone   706-657-4050
- ❑ Park Hours _____
- ❑ Reservations? ____Y ____N date made_____
- ❑ Open all year ____Y ____N dates_____
- ❑ Check in time _____
- ❑ Check out time _____
- ❑ Pet friendly ____Y ____N
- ❑ Max RV length _____
- ❑ Distance from home

  miles: _____

  hours: _____
- ❑ Address_____

Fees:

- ❑ Day Use $ _____
- ❑ Camp Sites $ _____
- ❑ RV Sites $ _____
- ❑ Refund policy _____

Make It Personal

Trip dates: _____ | The weather was: Sunny Cloudy Rainy Stormy Snowy Foggy Warm Cold

Why I went: _____

How I got there: (circle all that apply)   Plane   Train   Car   Bus   Bike   Hike   RV   MC

I went with: _____

We stayed in (space, cabin # etc): _____

Most relaxing day: _____

Something funny: _____

Someone we met: _____

Best story told: _____

The kids liked this: _____

The best food: _____

Games played: _____

Something disappointing: _____

Next time I'll do this differently: _____

Amicalola Falls State Park & Lodge

City: Dawsonville **County: Dawson**

Plan your trip: https://www.amicalolafallslodge.com/

Activities:

- ❑ Archery
- ❑ Biking Trails
- ❑ Boating
- ❑ Canoeing
- ❑ Canyon Climbing
- ❑ Caving
- ❑ Fishing
- ❑ Geocaching
- ❑ Hiking
- ❑ Historic Sites
- ❑ Horseback
- ❑ Hunting
- ❑ Kayaking
- ❑ Nature Programs
- ❑ Photography
- ❑ Rock Climbing
- ❑ Stargazing
- ❑ Swimming
- ❑ Water Skiing
- ❑ Wildlife & Bird Watching
- ❑ Ziplining

Facilities:

- ❑ ADA
- ❑ Picnic sites
- ❑ Restrooms
- ❑ Showers
- ❑ Trailer Access
- ❑ Visitor center
- ❑ Group Camping
- ❑ RV Camp
- ❑ Rustic Camping
- ❑ Cabins / Yurts
- ❑ Day Use Area

Notes:

Get the Facts

- ❑ Phone 800-573-9656
- ❑ Park Hours _____
- ❑ Reservations? ____Y ____N date made _____
- ❑ Open all year ____Y ____N dates _____
- ❑ Check in time _____
- ❑ Check out time _____
- ❑ Pet friendly ____Y ____N
- ❑ Max RV length _____
- ❑ Distance from home miles: _____ hours: _____
- ❑ Address _____ _____ _____

Fees:

- ❑ Day Use $ _____
- ❑ Camp Sites $ _____
- ❑ RV Sites $ _____
- ❑ Refund policy _____ _____ _____

Make It Personal

Trip dates: _____ | The weather was: Sunny   Cloudy   Rainy   Stormy   Snowy   Foggy   Warm   Cold

Why I went:
_____
_____

How I got there: (circle all that apply)   Plane   Train   Car   Bus   Bike   Hike   RV   MC

I went with:
_____

We stayed in (space, cabin # etc):
_____

Most relaxing day:
_____
_____

Something funny:
_____
_____

Someone we met:
_____
_____

Best story told:
_____
_____

The kids liked this:
_____

The best food:
_____

Games played:
_____

Something disappointing:
_____

Next time I'll do this differently:
_____
_____

Rocky Mountain Recreation & Public Fishing Area

City: Rome   County: Floyd

Plan your trip: https://georgiawildlife.com/rocky-mountain-pfa

Activities:

- ❑ Archery
- ❑ Biking Trails
- ❑ Boating
- ❑ Canoeing
- ❑ Canyon Climbing
- ❑ Caving
- ❑ Fishing
- ❑ Geocaching
- ❑ Hiking
- ❑ Historic Sites
- ❑ Horseback
- ❑ Hunting
- ❑ Kayaking
- ❑ Nature Programs
- ❑ Photography
- ❑ Rock Climbing
- ❑ Stargazing
- ❑ Swimming
- ❑ Water Skiing
- ❑ Wildlife & Bird Watching
- ❑ Ziplining

Facilities:

- ❑ ADA
- ❑ Picnic sites
- ❑ Restrooms
- ❑ Showers
- ❑ Trailer Access
- ❑ Visitor center
- ❑ Group Camping
- ❑ RV Camp
- ❑ Rustic Camping
- ❑ Cabins / Yurts
- ❑ Day Use Area

Notes:

Get the Facts

- ❑ Phone   706-802-5087
- ❑ Park Hours _____
- ❑ Reservations? ____Y ____N date made_____
- ❑ Open all year ____Y ____N dates_____
- ❑ Check in time _____
- ❑ Check out time _____
- ❑ Pet friendly _____Y _____N
- ❑ Max RV length _____
- ❑ Distance from home miles: _____ hours: _____
- ❑ Address_____

Fees:

- ❑ Day Use $ _____
- ❑ Camp Sites $ _____
- ❑ RV Sites $ _____
- ❑ Refund policy _____

Make It Personal

Trip dates: _____ | The weather was: Sunny Cloudy Rainy Stormy Snowy Foggy Warm Cold

Why I went: _____
_____

How I got there: (circle all that apply)   Plane   Train   Car   Bus   Bike   Hike   RV   MC

I went with: _____

We stayed in (space, cabin # etc): _____

Most relaxing day: _____
_____

Something funny: _____
_____

Someone we met: _____
_____

Best story told: _____
_____

The kids liked this: _____
_____

The best food: _____
_____

Games played: _____
_____

Something disappointing: _____
_____

Next time I'll do this differently: _____
_____

Fort Mountain State Park
City: Chatsworth   County: Murray
Plan your trip: https://gastateparks.org/FortMountain

Activities:

- ❏ Archery
- ❏ Biking Trails
- ❏ Boating
- ❏ Canoeing
- ❏ Canyon Climbing
- ❏ Caving
- ❏ Fishing
- ❏ Geocaching
- ❏ Hiking
- ❏ Historic Sites
- ❏ Horseback
- ❏ Hunting
- ❏ Kayaking
- ❏ Nature Programs
- ❏ Photography
- ❏ Rock Climbing
- ❏ Stargazing
- ❏ Swimming
- ❏ Water Skiing
- ❏ Wildlife & Bird Watching
- ❏ Ziplining

Facilities:

- ❏ ADA
- ❏ Picnic sites
- ❏ Restrooms
- ❏ Showers
- ❏ Trailer Access
- ❏ Visitor center
- ❏ Group Camping
- ❏ RV Camp
- ❏ Rustic Camping
- ❏ Cabins / Yurts
- ❏ Day Use Area

Notes:

Get the Facts

- ❏ Phone   706-422-1932
- ❏ Park Hours _____
- ❏ Reservations? ____Y ____N date made_____
- ❏ Open all year ____Y ____N dates_____
- ❏ Check in time _____
- ❏ Check out time _____
- ❏ Pet friendly ____Y ____N
- ❏ Max RV length _____
- ❏ Distance from home
   miles: _____
   hours: _____
- ❏ Address _____

Fees:

- ❏ Day Use $ _____
- ❏ Camp Sites $ _____
- ❏ RV Sites $ _____
- ❏ Refund policy _____

Make It Personal

Trip dates: _____ | The weather was: Sunny Cloudy Rainy Stormy Snowy Foggy Warm Cold

Why I went: _____
_____

How I got there: (circle all that apply) Plane Train Car Bus Bike Hike RV MC

I went with: _____

We stayed in (space, cabin # etc): _____

Most relaxing day: _____
_____

Something funny: _____
_____

Someone we met: _____
_____

Best story told: _____
_____

The kids liked this: _____
_____

The best food: _____
_____

Games played: _____
_____

Something disappointing: _____
_____

Next time I'll do this differently: _____
_____

Moccasin Creek State Park
City: Clarkesville   County: Rabun

Plan your trip: https://gastateparks.org/MoccasinCreek

Activities:

- ❑ Archery
- ❑ Biking Trails
- ❑ Boating
- ❑ Canoeing
- ❑ Canyon Climbing
- ❑ Caving
- ❑ Fishing
- ❑ Geocaching
- ❑ Hiking
- ❑ Historic Sites
- ❑ Horseback
- ❑ Hunting
- ❑ Kayaking
- ❑ Nature Programs
- ❑ Photography
- ❑ Rock Climbing
- ❑ Stargazing
- ❑ Swimming
- ❑ Water Skiing
- ❑ Wildlife & Bird Watching
- ❑ Ziplining

Facilities:

- ❑ ADA
- ❑ Picnic sites
- ❑ Restrooms
- ❑ Showers
- ❑ Trailer Access
- ❑ Visitor center
- ❑ Group Camping
- ❑ RV Camp
- ❑ Rustic Camping
- ❑ Cabins / Yurts
- ❑ Day Use Area

Notes:

Get the Facts

- ❑ Phone   706-947-3194
- ❑ Park Hours _____
- ❑ Reservations? ____Y ____N date made_____
- ❑ Open all year ____Y ____N dates_____
- ❑ Check in time _____
- ❑ Check out time _____
- ❑ Pet friendly ____Y ____N
- ❑ Max RV length _____
- ❑ Distance from home
  miles: _____
  hours: _____
- ❑ Address_____

Fees:

- ❑ Day Use $ _____
- ❑ Camp Sites $ _____
- ❑ RV Sites $ _____
- ❑ Refund policy _____

Make It Personal

Trip dates: _____ | The weather was: Sunny   Cloudy   Rainy   Stormy   Snowy   Foggy   Warm   Cold

Why I went:
_____
_____

How I got there: (circle all that apply)   Plane   Train   Car   Bus   Bike   Hike   RV   MC

I went with:
_____

We stayed in (space, cabin # etc):
_____

Most relaxing day:
_____
_____

Something funny:
_____
_____

Someone we met:
_____
_____

Best story told:
_____
_____

The kids liked this:
_____
_____

The best food:
_____
_____

Games played:
_____
_____

Something disappointing:
_____
_____

Next time I'll do this differently:
_____
_____

Black Rock Mountain State Park
City: Mountain City   County: Rabun

Plan your trip: https://gastateparks.org/BlackRockMountain

Activities:

- [ ] Archery
- [ ] Biking Trails
- [ ] Boating
- [ ] Canoeing
- [ ] Canyon Climbing
- [ ] Caving
- [ ] Fishing
- [ ] Geocaching
- [ ] Hiking
- [ ] Historic Sites
- [ ] Horseback
- [ ] Hunting
- [ ] Kayaking
- [ ] Nature Programs
- [ ] Photography
- [ ] Rock Climbing
- [ ] Stargazing
- [ ] Swimming
- [ ] Water Skiing
- [ ] Wildlife & Bird Watching
- [ ] Ziplining

Facilities:

- [ ] ADA
- [ ] Picnic sites
- [ ] Restrooms
- [ ] Showers
- [ ] Trailer Access
- [ ] Visitor center
- [ ] Group Camping
- [ ] RV Camp
- [ ] Rustic Camping
- [ ] Cabins / Yurts
- [ ] Day Use Area

Notes:

Get the Facts

- [ ] Phone   706-746-2141
- [ ] Park Hours _____
- [ ] Reservations? ____Y ____N date made_____
- [ ] Open all year ____Y ____N dates_____
- [ ] Check in time _____
- [ ] Check out time _____
- [ ] Pet friendly _____Y _____N
- [ ] Max RV length _____
- [ ] Distance from home
  miles: _____
  hours: _____
- [ ] Address_____ _____ _____

Fees:

- [ ] Day Use $ _____
- [ ] Camp Sites $ _____
- [ ] RV Sites $ _____
- [ ] Refund policy _____ _____ _____

Make It Personal

Trip dates: _____ | The weather was: Sunny Cloudy Rainy Stormy Snowy Foggy Warm Cold

Why I went:
_____
_____

How I got there: (circle all that apply)   Plane   Train   Car   Bus   Bike   Hike   RV   MC
_____

I went with:
_____

We stayed in (space, cabin # etc):
_____

Most relaxing day:
_____
_____

Something funny:
_____
_____

Someone we met:
_____
_____

Best story told:
_____
_____

The kids liked this:
_____
_____

The best food:
_____
_____

Games played:
_____
_____

Something disappointing:
_____
_____

Next time I'll do this differently:
_____
_____

Tallulah Gorge State Park
City: Tallulah Falls　　　County: Habersham

Plan your trip: https://gastateparks.org/TallulahGorge

Activities:

- ❑ Archery
- ❑ Biking Trails
- ❑ Boating
- ❑ Canoeing
- ❑ Canyon Climbing
- ❑ Caving
- ❑ Fishing
- ❑ Geocaching
- ❑ Hiking
- ❑ Historic Sites
- ❑ Horseback
- ❑ Hunting
- ❑ Kayaking
- ❑ Nature Programs
- ❑ Photography
- ❑ Rock Climbing
- ❑ Stargazing
- ❑ Swimming
- ❑ Water Skiing
- ❑ Wildlife & Bird Watching
- ❑ Ziplining

Facilities:

- ❑ ADA
- ❑ Picnic sites
- ❑ Restrooms
- ❑ Showers
- ❑ Trailer Access
- ❑ Visitor center
- ❑ Group Camping
- ❑ RV Camp
- ❑ Rustic Camping
- ❑ Cabins / Yurts
- ❑ Day Use Area

Notes:

Get the Facts

- ❑ Phone   706-754-7981
- ❑ Park Hours _____
- ❑ Reservations? ____Y ____N date made_____
- ❑ Open all year ____Y ____N dates_____
- ❑ Check in time _____
- ❑ Check out time _____
- ❑ Pet friendly ____Y ____N
- ❑ Max RV length _____
- ❑ Distance from home miles: _____ hours: _____
- ❑ Address _____

Fees:

- ❑ Day Use $ _____
- ❑ Camp Sites $ _____
- ❑ RV Sites $ _____
- ❑ Refund policy _____

Make It Personal

Trip dates: _____ | The weather was: Sunny Cloudy Rainy Stormy Snowy Foggy Warm Cold

Why I went:
_____
_____

How I got there: (circle all that apply)   Plane   Train   Car   Bus   Bike   Hike   RV   MC
_____

I went with:
_____

We stayed in (space, cabin # etc):
_____

Most relaxing day:
_____
_____

Something funny:
_____
_____

Someone we met:
_____
_____

Best story told:
_____
_____

The kids liked this:
_____
_____

The best food:
_____
_____

Games played:
_____
_____

Something disappointing:
_____
_____

Next time I'll do this differently:
_____
_____

Vogel State Park
City: Blairsville   County: Union
Plan your trip: https://gastateparks.org/Vogel

Activities:

- ❏ Archery
- ❏ Biking Trails
- ❏ Boating
- ❏ Canoeing
- ❏ Canyon Climbing
- ❏ Caving
- ❏ Fishing
- ❏ Geocaching
- ❏ Hiking
- ❏ Historic Sites
- ❏ Horseback
- ❏ Hunting
- ❏ Kayaking
- ❏ Nature Programs
- ❏ Photography
- ❏ Rock Climbing
- ❏ Stargazing
- ❏ Swimming
- ❏ Water Skiing
- ❏ Wildlife & Bird Watching
- ❏ Ziplining

Facilities:

- ❏ ADA
- ❏ Picnic sites
- ❏ Restrooms
- ❏ Showers
- ❏ Trailer Access
- ❏ Visitor center
- ❏ Group Camping
- ❏ RV Camp
- ❏ Rustic Camping
- ❏ Cabins / Yurts
- ❏ Day Use Area

Notes:

Get the Facts

- ❏ Phone   706-745-2628
- ❏ Park Hours _____
- ❏ Reservations? ____Y ____N date made_____
- ❏ Open all year ____Y ____N dates_____
- ❏ Check in time _____
- ❏ Check out time _____
- ❏ Pet friendly ____Y ____N
- ❏ Max RV length _____
- ❏ Distance from home miles: _____ hours: _____
- ❏ Address _____

Fees:

- ❏ Day Use $ _____
- ❏ Camp Sites $ _____
- ❏ RV Sites $ _____
- ❏ Refund policy _____

Make It Personal

Trip dates: _____ | The weather was: Sunny Cloudy Rainy Stormy Snowy Foggy Warm Cold

Why I went: _____

How I got there: (circle all that apply)   Plane   Train   Car   Bus   Bike   Hike   RV   MC

I went with: _____

We stayed in (space, cabin # etc): _____

Most relaxing day: _____

Something funny: _____

Someone we met: _____

Best story told: _____

The kids liked this: _____

The best food: _____

Games played: _____

Something disappointing: _____

Next time I'll do this differently: _____

Smithgall Woods State Park
City: Helen   County: White

Plan your trip: https://gastateparks.org/SmithgallWoods

Activities:

- ❑ Archery
- ❑ Biking Trails
- ❑ Boating
- ❑ Canoeing
- ❑ Canyon Climbing
- ❑ Caving
- ❑ Fishing
- ❑ Geocaching
- ❑ Hiking
- ❑ Historic Sites
- ❑ Horseback
- ❑ Hunting
- ❑ Kayaking
- ❑ Nature Programs
- ❑ Photography
- ❑ Rock Climbing
- ❑ Stargazing
- ❑ Swimming
- ❑ Water Skiing
- ❑ Wildlife & Bird Watching
- ❑ Ziplining

Facilities:

- ❑ ADA
- ❑ Picnic sites
- ❑ Restrooms
- ❑ Showers
- ❑ Trailer Access
- ❑ Visitor center
- ❑ Group Camping
- ❑ RV Camp
- ❑ Rustic Camping
- ❑ Cabins / Yurts
- ❑ Day Use Area

Notes:

Get the Facts

- ❑ Phone   706-878-3087
- ❑ Park Hours _____
- ❑ Reservations? ____Y ____N date made_____
- ❑ Open all year ____Y ____N dates_____
- ❑ Check in time _____
- ❑ Check out time _____
- ❑ Pet friendly ____Y ____N
- ❑ Max RV length _____
- ❑ Distance from home
  miles: _____
  hours: _____
- ❑ Address_____

Fees:

- ❑ Day Use $ _____
- ❑ Camp Sites $ _____
- ❑ RV Sites $ _____
- ❑ Refund policy _____

Make It Personal

Trip dates: _____ | The weather was: Sunny   Cloudy   Rainy   Stormy   Snowy   Foggy   Warm   Cold

Why I went:
_____

How I got there: (circle all that apply)   Plane   Train   Car   Bus   Bike   Hike   RV   MC

I went with:
_____

We stayed in (space, cabin # etc):
_____

Most relaxing day:
_____

Something funny:
_____

Someone we met:
_____

Best story told:
_____

The kids liked this:
_____

The best food:
_____

Games played:
_____

Something disappointing:
_____

Next time I'll do this differently:
_____
_____

Unicoi State Park & Lodge
City: Helen   **County: White**

Plan your trip: https://www.unicoilodge.com/

Activities:

- ❑ Archery
- ❑ Biking Trails
- ❑ Boating
- ❑ Canoeing
- ❑ Canyon Climbing
- ❑ Caving
- ❑ Fishing
- ❑ Geocaching
- ❑ Hiking
- ❑ Historic Sites
- ❑ Horseback
- ❑ Hunting
- ❑ Kayaking
- ❑ Nature Programs
- ❑ Photography
- ❑ Rock Climbing
- ❑ Stargazing
- ❑ Swimming
- ❑ Water Skiing
- ❑ Wildlife & Bird Watching
- ❑ Ziplining

Facilities:

- ❑ ADA
- ❑ Picnic sites
- ❑ Restrooms
- ❑ Showers
- ❑ Trailer Access
- ❑ Visitor center
- ❑ Group Camping
- ❑ RV Camp
- ❑ Rustic Camping
- ❑ Cabins / Yurts
- ❑ Day Use Area

Notes:

Get the Facts

- ❑ Phone   800-573-9658
- ❑ Park Hours _____
- ❑ Reservations? ____Y ____N date made_____
- ❑ Open all year ____Y ____N dates_____
- ❑ Check in time _____
- ❑ Check out time _____
- ❑ Pet friendly ____Y ____N
- ❑ Max RV length _____
- ❑ Distance from home
  miles: _____
  hours: _____
- ❑ Address_____

Fees:

- ❑ Day Use $ _____
- ❑ Camp Sites $ _____
- ❑ RV Sites $ _____
- ❑ Refund policy _____

Make It Personal

Trip dates: _____ | The weather was: Sunny Cloudy Rainy Stormy Snowy Foggy Warm Cold

Why I went: _____
_____

How I got there: (circle all that apply)   Plane   Train   Car   Bus   Bike   Hike   RV   MC

I went with: _____

We stayed in (space, cabin # etc): _____

Most relaxing day: _____
_____

Something funny: _____
_____

Someone we met: _____
_____

Best story told: _____
_____

The kids liked this: _____
_____

The best food: _____
_____

Games played: _____
_____

Something disappointing: _____
_____

Next time I'll do this differently: _____
_____

Etowah Indian Mounds State Historic Site

City: Cartersville **County: Bartow**

Plan your trip: https://gastateparks.org/EtowahIndianMounds

Activities:

- ❑ Bike Trails ❑
- ❑ Bird Watching ❑
- ❑ Boating ❑
- ❑ Fishing ❑
- ❑ Hiking ❑
- ❑ Historic Site ❑
- ❑ Hunting ❑
- ❑ Geocaching ❑
- ❑ Nature Trails ❑
- ❑ Watersports ❑
- ❑ Wildlife Viewing ❑

Facilities:

- ❑ ADA ❑
- ❑ Gift Shop ❑
- ❑ Museum ❑
- ❑ Visitor Center ❑
- ❑ Picnic sites ❑
- ❑ Restrooms ❑

Things to do in the area:

Get the Facts

- ❑ Phone 770-387-3747
- ❑ Park Hours _____
- ❑ Reservations? ____Y ____N date made_____
- ❑ Open all year? ____Y ____N dates_____
- ❑ Dog friendly ____Y ____N
- ❑ Distance from home

  miles: _____

  hours: _____
- ❑ Address_____ _____ _____

Fees:

- ❑ Day Use $ _____
- ❑ Refund policy _____ _____ _____

Notes:

New Echota State Historic Site
City: Calhoun   County: Gordon

Plan your trip: https://gastateparks.org/NewEchota

Activities:

- ❑ Bike Trails ❑
- ❑ Bird Watching ❑
- ❑ Boating ❑
- ❑ Fishing ❑
- ❑ Hiking ❑
- ❑ Historic Site ❑
- ❑ Hunting ❑
- ❑ Geocaching ❑
- ❑ Nature Trails ❑
- ❑ Watersports ❑
- ❑ Wildlife Viewing ❑

Facilities:

- ❑ ADA ❑
- ❑ Gift Shop ❑
- ❑ Museum ❑
- ❑ Visitor Center ❑
- ❑ Picnic sites ❑
- ❑ Restrooms ❑

Things to do in the area:

Get the Facts

- ❑ Phone 706-624-1321
- ❑ Park Hours _____
- ❑ Reservations? ____Y ____N
  date made_____
- ❑ Open all year? ____Y ____N
  dates_____
- ❑ Dog friendly ____Y ____N
- ❑ Distance from home
  miles: _____
  hours: _____
- ❑ Address_____
  _____
  _____

Fees:

- ❑ Day Use $ _____
- ❑ Refund policy
  _____
  _____
  _____

Notes:

Resaca Battlefield

City: Resaca   **County: Gordon**

Plan your trip: http://www.gordoncountyparks.org/#RBHStop

Activities:

- ❏ Bike Trails
- ❏ Bird Watching
- ❏ Boating
- ❏ Fishing
- ❏ Hiking
- ❏ Historic Site
- ❏ Hunting
- ❏ Geocaching
- ❏ Nature Trails
- ❏ Watersports
- ❏ Wildlife Viewing

Facilities:

- ❏ ADA
- ❏ Gift Shop
- ❏ Museum
- ❏ Visitor Center
- ❏ Picnic sites
- ❏ Restrooms

Things to do in the area:

Get the Facts

- ❏ Phone 706-629-4435
- ❏ Park Hours _____
- ❏ Reservations? ____Y ____N date made_____
- ❏ Open all year? ____Y ____N dates_____
- ❏ Dog friendly ____Y ____N
- ❏ Distance from home
  miles: _____
  hours: _____
- ❏ Address_____

Fees:

- ❏ Day Use $ _____
- ❏ Refund policy _____

Notes:

Dahlonega Gold Museum State Historic Site

City: Dahlonega **County: Lumpkin**

Plan your trip: https://gastateparks.org/DahlonegaGoldMuseum

Activities:

- ❏ Bike Trails ❏
- ❏ Bird Watching ❏
- ❏ Boating ❏
- ❏ Fishing ❏
- ❏ Hiking ❏
- ❏ Historic Site ❏
- ❏ Hunting ❏
- ❏ Geocaching ❏
- ❏ Nature Trails ❏
- ❏ Watersports ❏
- ❏ Wildlife Viewing ❏

Facilities:

- ❏ ADA ❏
- ❏ Gift Shop ❏
- ❏ Museum ❏
- ❏ Visitor Center ❏
- ❏ Picnic sites ❏
- ❏ Restrooms ❏

Things to do in the area:

Get the Facts

- ❏ Phone 706-864-2257
- ❏ Park Hours _____
- ❏ Reservations? ____Y ____N date made_____
- ❏ Open all year? ____Y ____N dates_____
- ❏ Dog friendly ____Y ____N
- ❏ Distance from home
  miles: _____
  hours: _____
- ❏ Address_____
  _____
  _____

Fees:

- ❏ Day Use $ _____
- ❏ Refund policy
  _____
  _____
  _____

Notes:

Chief Vann House State Historic Site
City: Chatsworth **County: Murray**

Plan your trip: https://gastateparks.org/ChiefVannHouse

Activities:

- ❑ Bike Trails ❑
- ❑ Bird Watching ❑
- ❑ Boating ❑
- ❑ Fishing ❑
- ❑ Hiking ❑
- ❑ Historic Site ❑
- ❑ Hunting ❑
- ❑ Geocaching ❑
- ❑ Nature Trails ❑
- ❑ Watersports ❑
- ❑ Wildlife Viewing ❑

Facilities:

- ❑ ADA ❑
- ❑ Gift Shop ❑
- ❑ Museum ❑
- ❑ Visitor Center ❑
- ❑ Picnic sites ❑
- ❑ Restrooms ❑

Things to do in the area:

Get the Facts

- ❑ Phone 706-695-2598
- ❑ Park Hours _____
- ❑ Reservations? ____Y ____N date made_____
- ❑ Open all year? ____Y ____N dates_____
- ❑ Dog friendly ____Y ____N
- ❑ Distance from home
  miles: _____
  hours: _____
- ❑ Address_____
  _____
  _____

Fees:

- ❑ Day Use $ _____
- ❑ Refund policy
  _____
  _____
  _____

Notes:

Pickett's Mill Battlefield State Historic Site

City: Dallas **County: Paulding**

Plan your trip: https://gastateparks.org/PickettsMillBattlefield

Activities:

- ❑ Bike Trails ❑
- ❑ Bird Watching ❑
- ❑ Boating ❑
- ❑ Fishing ❑
- ❑ Hiking ❑
- ❑ Historic Site ❑
- ❑ Hunting ❑
- ❑ Geocaching ❑
- ❑ Nature Trails ❑
- ❑ Watersports ❑
- ❑ Wildlife Viewing ❑

Facilities:

- ❑ ADA ❑
- ❑ Gift Shop ❑
- ❑ Museum ❑
- ❑ Visitor Center ❑
- ❑ Picnic sites ❑
- ❑ Restrooms ❑

Things to do in the area:

Get the Facts

- ❑ Phone 770-443-7850
- ❑ Park Hours _____
- ❑ Reservations? ____Y ____N date made_____
- ❑ Open all year? ____Y ____N dates_____
- ❑ Dog friendly ____Y ____N
- ❑ Distance from home
  miles: _____
  hours: _____
- ❑ Address_____ _____ _____

Fees:

- ❑ Day Use $ _____
- ❑ Refund policy _____ _____ _____

Notes:

37

Hardman Farm State Historic Site
City: Sautee Nacoochee   County: White

Plan your trip: https://gastateparks.org/HardmanFarm

Activities:

- ❑ Bike Trails ❑
- ❑ Bird Watching ❑
- ❑ Boating ❑
- ❑ Fishing ❑
- ❑ Hiking ❑
- ❑ Historic Site ❑
- ❑ Hunting ❑
- ❑ Geocaching ❑
- ❑ Nature Trails ❑
- ❑ Watersports ❑
- ❑ Wildlife Viewing ❑

Facilities:

- ❑ ADA ❑
- ❑ Gift Shop ❑
- ❑ Museum ❑
- ❑ Visitor Center ❑
- ❑ Picnic sites ❑
- ❑ Restrooms ❑

Things to do in the area:

Get the Facts

- ❑ Phone 706-878-1077
- ❑ Park Hours _____
- ❑ Reservations? ____Y ____N
  date made_____
- ❑ Open all year? ____Y____N
  dates_____
- ❑ Dog friendly ____Y ____N
- ❑ Distance from home
  miles: _____
  hours: _____
- ❑ Address_____
  _____
  _____

Fees:

- ❑ Day Use $ _____
- ❑ Refund policy
  _____
  _____
  _____

Notes:

38

Fort Yargo State Park
City: Winder   County: Barrow
Plan your trip: https://gastateparks.org/FortYargo

Activities:

- ❑ Archery
- ❑ Biking Trails
- ❑ Boating
- ❑ Canoeing
- ❑ Canyon Climbing
- ❑ Caving
- ❑ Fishing
- ❑ Geocaching
- ❑ Hiking
- ❑ Historic Sites
- ❑ Horseback
- ❑ Hunting
- ❑ Kayaking
- ❑ Nature Programs
- ❑ Photography
- ❑ Rock Climbing
- ❑ Stargazing
- ❑ Swimming
- ❑ Water Skiing
- ❑ Wildlife & Bird Watching
- ❑ Ziplining

Facilities:

- ❑ ADA
- ❑ Picnic sites
- ❑ Restrooms
- ❑ Showers
- ❑ Trailer Access
- ❑ Visitor center
- ❑ Group Camping
- ❑ RV Camp
- ❑ Rustic Camping
- ❑ Cabins / Yurts
- ❑ Day Use Area

Notes:

Get the Facts

- ❑ Phone   770-867-3489
- ❑ Park Hours _____
- ❑ Reservations? ____Y ____N date made_____
- ❑ Open all year ____Y ____N dates_____
- ❑ Check in time _____
- ❑ Check out time _____
- ❑ Pet friendly ____Y ____N
- ❑ Max RV length _____
- ❑ Distance from home miles: _____ hours: _____
- ❑ Address _____

Fees:

- ❑ Day Use $ _____
- ❑ Camp Sites $ _____
- ❑ RV Sites $ _____
- ❑ Refund policy _____

Make It Personal

Trip dates: _____ | The weather was: Sunny   Cloudy   Rainy   Stormy   Snowy   Foggy   Warm   Cold

Why I went:
_____

How I got there: (circle all that apply)   Plane   Train   Car   Bus   Bike   Hike   RV   MC

I went with:
_____

We stayed in (space, cabin # etc):
_____

Most relaxing day:
_____

Something funny:
_____

Someone we met:
_____

Best story told:
_____

The kids liked this:
_____

The best food:
_____

Games played:
_____

Something disappointing:
_____

Next time I'll do this differently:
_____

Indian Springs State Park

City: Flovilla   **County: Butts**

Plan your trip: https://gastateparks.org/IndianSprings

Activities:

- ☐ Archery
- ☐ Biking Trails
- ☐ Boating
- ☐ Canoeing
- ☐ Canyon Climbing
- ☐ Caving
- ☐ Fishing
- ☐ Geocaching
- ☐ Hiking
- ☐ Historic Sites
- ☐ Horseback
- ☐ Hunting
- ☐ Kayaking
- ☐ Nature Programs
- ☐ Photography
- ☐ Rock Climbing
- ☐ Stargazing
- ☐ Swimming
- ☐ Water Skiing
- ☐ Wildlife & Bird Watching
- ☐ Ziplining
- ☐
- ☐
- ☐
- ☐
- ☐
- ☐
- ☐
- ☐
- ☐
- ☐

Facilities:

- ☐ ADA
- ☐ Picnic sites
- ☐ Restrooms
- ☐ Showers
- ☐ Trailer Access
- ☐ Visitor center
- ☐ Group Camping
- ☐ RV Camp
- ☐ Rustic Camping
- ☐ Cabins / Yurts
- ☐ Day Use Area

Notes:

Get the Facts

- ☐ Phone   770-504-2277
- ☐ Park Hours _____
- ☐ Reservations? ____Y ____N date made_____
- ☐ Open all year ____Y ____N dates_____
- ☐ Check in time _____
- ☐ Check out time _____
- ☐ Pet friendly ____Y ____N
- ☐ Max RV length _____
- ☐ Distance from home miles: _____ hours: _____
- ☐ Address_____

Fees:

- ☐ Day Use $ _____
- ☐ Camp Sites $ _____
- ☐ RV Sites $ _____
- ☐ Refund policy _____

Make It Personal

Trip dates: _____ | The weather was: Sunny   Cloudy   Rainy   Stormy   Snowy   Foggy   Warm   Cold

Why I went: _____
_____

How I got there: (circle all that apply)   Plane   Train   Car   Bus   Bike   Hike   RV   MC

I went with: _____

We stayed in (space, cabin # etc): _____

Most relaxing day: _____
_____

Something funny: _____
_____

Someone we met: _____
_____

Best story told: _____
_____

The kids liked this: _____
_____

The best food: _____
_____

Games played: _____
_____

Something disappointing: _____
_____

Next time I'll do this differently: _____
_____

Mistletoe State Park

City: Appling **County: Columbia**

Plan your trip: https://gastateparks.org/Mistletoe

Activities:

- ❑ Archery
- ❑ Biking Trails
- ❑ Boating
- ❑ Canoeing
- ❑ Canyon Climbing
- ❑ Caving
- ❑ Fishing
- ❑ Geocaching
- ❑ Hiking
- ❑ Historic Sites
- ❑ Horseback
- ❑ Hunting
- ❑ Kayaking
- ❑ Nature Programs
- ❑ Photography
- ❑ Rock Climbing
- ❑ Stargazing
- ❑ Swimming
- ❑ Water Skiing
- ❑ Wildlife & Bird Watching
- ❑ Ziplining

Facilities:

- ❑ ADA
- ❑ Picnic sites
- ❑ Restrooms
- ❑ Showers
- ❑ Trailer Access
- ❑ Visitor center
- ❑ Group Camping
- ❑ RV Camp
- ❑ Rustic Camping
- ❑ Cabins / Yurts
- ❑ Day Use Area

Notes:

Get the Facts

- ❑ Phone   706-541-0321
- ❑ Park Hours _____
- ❑ Reservations? ____Y ____N date made_____
- ❑ Open all year ____Y ____N dates_____
- ❑ Check in time _____
- ❑ Check out time _____
- ❑ Pet friendly _____Y _____N
- ❑ Max RV length _____
- ❑ Distance from home miles: _____ hours: _____
- ❑ Address_____

Fees:

- ❑ Day Use $ _____
- ❑ Camp Sites $ _____
- ❑ RV Sites $ _____
- ❑ Refund policy _____

Make It Personal

Trip dates: _____ | The weather was: Sunny   Cloudy   Rainy   Stormy   Snowy   Foggy   Warm   Cold

Why I went:
_____

_____

How I got there: (circle all that apply)   Plane   Train   Car   Bus   Bike   Hike   RV   MC
_____

I went with:
_____

We stayed in (space, cabin # etc):
_____

Most relaxing day:
_____

_____

Something funny:
_____

_____

Someone we met:
_____

_____

Best story told:
_____

_____

The kids liked this:
_____

_____

The best food:
_____

_____

Games played:
_____

_____

Something disappointing:
_____

_____

Next time I'll do this differently:
_____

_____

_____

Chattahoochee Bend State Park

City: Newnan   **County: Coweta**

Plan your trip: https://gastateparks.org/ChattahoocheeBend

Activities:

- ❏ Archery
- ❏ Biking Trails
- ❏ Boating
- ❏ Canoeing
- ❏ Canyon Climbing
- ❏ Caving
- ❏ Fishing
- ❏ Geocaching
- ❏ Hiking
- ❏ Historic Sites
- ❏ Horseback
- ❏ Hunting
- ❏ Kayaking
- ❏ Nature Programs
- ❏ Photography
- ❏ Rock Climbing
- ❏ Stargazing
- ❏ Swimming
- ❏ Water Skiing
- ❏ Wildlife & Bird Watching
- ❏ Ziplining

Facilities:

- ❏ ADA
- ❏ Picnic sites
- ❏ Restrooms
- ❏ Showers
- ❏ Trailer Access
- ❏ Visitor center
- ❏ Group Camping
- ❏ RV Camp
- ❏ Rustic Camping
- ❏ Cabins / Yurts
- ❏ Day Use Area

Notes:

Get the Facts

- ❏ Phone   770-254-7271
- ❏ Park Hours _____
- ❏ Reservations? ____Y ____N date made_____
- ❏ Open all year ____Y ____N dates_____
- ❏ Check in time _____
- ❏ Check out time _____
- ❏ Pet friendly _____Y _____N
- ❏ Max RV length _____
- ❏ Distance from home
  miles: _____
  hours: _____
- ❏ Address_____

Fees:

- ❏ Day Use $ _____
- ❏ Camp Sites $ _____
- ❏ RV Sites $ _____
- ❏ Refund policy _____

Make It Personal

Trip dates: _____ | The weather was: Sunny Cloudy Rainy Stormy Snowy Foggy Warm Cold

Why I went:
_____

How I got there: (circle all that apply) Plane Train Car Bus Bike Hike RV MC

I went with:
_____

We stayed in (space, cabin # etc):
_____

Most relaxing day:
_____

Something funny:
_____

Someone we met:
_____

Best story told:
_____

The kids liked this:
_____

The best food:
_____

Games played:
_____

Something disappointing:
_____

Next time I'll do this differently:
_____
_____

Sweetwater Creek State Park
City: Lithia Springs   County: Douglas

Plan your trip: https://gastateparks.org/SweetwaterCreek

Activities:

- ☐ Archery
- ☐ Biking Trails
- ☐ Boating
- ☐ Canoeing
- ☐ Canyon Climbing
- ☐ Caving
- ☐ Fishing
- ☐ Geocaching
- ☐ Hiking
- ☐ Historic Sites
- ☐ Horseback
- ☐ Hunting
- ☐ Kayaking
- ☐ Nature Programs
- ☐ Photography
- ☐ Rock Climbing
- ☐ Stargazing
- ☐ Swimming
- ☐ Water Skiing
- ☐ Wildlife & Bird Watching
- ☐ Ziplining

Facilities:

- ☐ ADA
- ☐ Picnic sites
- ☐ Restrooms
- ☐ Showers
- ☐ Trailer Access
- ☐ Visitor center
- ☐ Group Camping
- ☐ RV Camp
- ☐ Rustic Camping
- ☐ Cabins / Yurts
- ☐ Day Use Area

Notes:

Get the Facts

- ☐ Phone   770-732-5871
- ☐ Park Hours _____
- ☐ Reservations? ____Y ____N date made_____
- ☐ Open all year ____Y ____N dates_____
- ☐ Check in time _____
- ☐ Check out time _____
- ☐ Pet friendly ____Y ____N
- ☐ Max RV length _____
- ☐ Distance from home miles: _____ hours: _____
- ☐ Address _____

Fees:

- ☐ Day Use $ _____
- ☐ Camp Sites $ _____
- ☐ RV Sites $ _____
- ☐ Refund policy _____

Make It Personal

Trip dates: _____ | The weather was: Sunny   Cloudy   Rainy   Stormy   Snowy   Foggy   Warm   Cold

Why I went:
_____

How I got there: (circle all that apply)   Plane   Train   Car   Bus   Bike   Hike   RV   MC

I went with:
_____

We stayed in (space, cabin # etc):
_____

Most relaxing day:
_____

Something funny:
_____

Someone we met:
_____

Best story told:
_____

The kids liked this:
_____

The best food:
_____

Games played:
_____

Something disappointing:
_____

Next time I'll do this differently:
_____
_____

Richard B. Russell State Park
City: Elberton   County: Elbert

Plan your trip: https://gastateparks.org/RichardBRussell

Activities:

- ❑ Archery
- ❑ Biking Trails
- ❑ Boating
- ❑ Canoeing
- ❑ Canyon Climbing
- ❑ Caving
- ❑ Fishing
- ❑ Geocaching
- ❑ Hiking
- ❑ Historic Sites
- ❑ Horseback
- ❑ Hunting
- ❑ Kayaking
- ❑ Nature Programs
- ❑ Photography
- ❑ Rock Climbing
- ❑ Stargazing
- ❑ Swimming
- ❑ Water Skiing
- ❑ Wildlife & Bird Watching
- ❑ Ziplining

Facilities:

- ❑ ADA
- ❑ Picnic sites
- ❑ Restrooms
- ❑ Showers
- ❑ Trailer Access
- ❑ Visitor center
- ❑ Group Camping
- ❑ RV Camp
- ❑ Rustic Camping
- ❑ Cabins / Yurts
- ❑ Day Use Area

Notes:

Get the Facts

- ❑ Phone   706-213-2045
- ❑ Park Hours _____
- ❑ Reservations? ____Y ____N date made_____
- ❑ Open all year ____Y ____N dates_____
- ❑ Check in time _____
- ❑ Check out time _____
- ❑ Pet friendly _____Y _____N
- ❑ Max RV length _____
- ❑ Distance from home
  miles: _____
  hours: _____
- ❑ Address_____ _____ _____

Fees:

- ❑ Day Use $ _____
- ❑ Camp Sites $ _____
- ❑ RV Sites $ _____
- ❑ Refund policy _____ _____ _____

Make It Personal

Trip dates: _____ | The weather was: Sunny   Cloudy   Rainy   Stormy   Snowy   Foggy   Warm   Cold

Why I went: _____
_____

How I got there: (circle all that apply)   Plane   Train   Car   Bus   Bike   Hike   RV   MC
_____

I went with: _____

We stayed in (space, cabin # etc): _____

Most relaxing day: _____
_____

Something funny: _____
_____

Someone we met: _____
_____

Best story told: _____
_____

The kids liked this: _____
_____

The best food: _____
_____

Games played: _____
_____

Something disappointing: _____
_____

Next time I'll do this differently: _____
_____

Tugaloo State Park
City: Lavonia   County: Franklin
Plan your trip: https://gastateparks.org/Tugaloo

Activities:

- ❑ Archery
- ❑ Biking Trails
- ❑ Boating
- ❑ Canoeing
- ❑ Canyon Climbing
- ❑ Caving
- ❑ Fishing
- ❑ Geocaching
- ❑ Hiking
- ❑ Historic Sites
- ❑ Horseback
- ❑ Hunting
- ❑ Kayaking
- ❑ Nature Programs
- ❑ Photography
- ❑ Rock Climbing
- ❑ Stargazing
- ❑ Swimming
- ❑ Water Skiing
- ❑ Wildlife & Bird Watching
- ❑ Ziplining

Facilities:

- ❑ ADA
- ❑ Picnic sites
- ❑ Restrooms
- ❑ Showers
- ❑ Trailer Access
- ❑ Visitor center
- ❑ Group Camping
- ❑ RV Camp
- ❑ Rustic Camping
- ❑ Cabins / Yurts
- ❑ Day Use Area

Notes:

Get the Facts

- ❑ Phone   706-356-4362
- ❑ Park Hours _____
- ❑ Reservations? ____Y ____N date made_____
- ❑ Open all year ____Y ____N dates_____
- ❑ Check in time _____
- ❑ Check out time _____
- ❑ Pet friendly _____Y _____N
- ❑ Max RV length _____
- ❑ Distance from home miles: _____ hours: _____
- ❑ Address_____

Fees:

- ❑ Day Use $ _____
- ❑ Camp Sites $ _____
- ❑ RV Sites $ _____
- ❑ Refund policy _____

Make It Personal

Trip dates: _____ | The weather was: Sunny   Cloudy   Rainy   Stormy   Snowy   Foggy   Warm   Cold

Why I went:
_____
_____

How I got there: (circle all that apply)   Plane   Train   Car   Bus   Bike   Hike   RV   MC
_____

I went with:
_____

We stayed in (space, cabin # etc):
_____

Most relaxing day:
_____
_____

Something funny:
_____
_____

Someone we met:
_____
_____

Best story told:
_____
_____

The kids liked this:
_____
_____

The best food:
_____
_____

Games played:
_____
_____

Something disappointing:
_____
_____

Next time I'll do this differently:
_____
_____

Victoria Bryant State Park
City: Royston County: Franklin

Plan your trip: https://gastateparks.org/VictoriaBryant

Activities:

- ❑ Archery
- ❑ Biking Trails
- ❑ Boating
- ❑ Canoeing
- ❑ Canyon Climbing
- ❑ Caving
- ❑ Fishing
- ❑ Geocaching
- ❑ Hiking
- ❑ Historic Sites
- ❑ Horseback
- ❑ Hunting
- ❑ Kayaking
- ❑ Nature Programs
- ❑ Photography
- ❑ Rock Climbing
- ❑ Stargazing
- ❑ Swimming
- ❑ Water Skiing
- ❑ Wildlife & Bird Watching
- ❑ Ziplining

Facilities:

- ❑ ADA
- ❑ Picnic sites
- ❑ Restrooms
- ❑ Showers
- ❑ Trailer Access
- ❑ Visitor center
- ❑ Group Camping
- ❑ RV Camp
- ❑ Rustic Camping
- ❑ Cabins / Yurts
- ❑ Day Use Area

Notes:

Get the Facts

- ❑ Phone 706-245-6270
- ❑ Park Hours _____
- ❑ Reservations? ____Y ____N date made_____
- ❑ Open all year ____Y ____N dates_____
- ❑ Check in time _____
- ❑ Check out time _____
- ❑ Pet friendly ____Y ____N
- ❑ Max RV length _____
- ❑ Distance from home miles: _____ hours: _____
- ❑ Address _____

Fees:

- ❑ Day Use $ _____
- ❑ Camp Sites $ _____
- ❑ RV Sites $ _____
- ❑ Refund policy _____

Make It Personal

Trip dates: The weather was: Sunny   Cloudy   Rainy   Stormy   Snowy   Foggy   Warm   Cold

Why I went:

How I got there: (circle all that apply)   Plane   Train   Car   Bus   Bike   Hike   RV   MC

I went with:

We stayed in (space, cabin # etc):

Most relaxing day:

Something funny:

Someone we met:

Best story told:

The kids liked this:

The best food:

Games played:

Something disappointing:

Next time I'll do this differently:

Don Carter State Park
City: Gainesville County: Hall
Plan your trip: https://gastateparks.org/DonCarter

Activities:

- ❑ Archery
- ❑ Biking Trails
- ❑ Boating
- ❑ Canoeing
- ❑ Canyon Climbing
- ❑ Caving
- ❑ Fishing
- ❑ Geocaching
- ❑ Hiking
- ❑ Historic Sites
- ❑ Horseback
- ❑ Hunting
- ❑ Kayaking
- ❑ Nature Programs
- ❑ Photography
- ❑ Rock Climbing
- ❑ Stargazing
- ❑ Swimming
- ❑ Water Skiing
- ❑ Wildlife & Bird Watching
- ❑ Ziplining

Facilities:

- ❑ ADA
- ❑ Picnic sites
- ❑ Restrooms
- ❑ Showers
- ❑ Trailer Access
- ❑ Visitor center
- ❑ Group Camping
- ❑ RV Camp
- ❑ Rustic Camping
- ❑ Cabins / Yurts
- ❑ Day Use Area

Notes:

Get the Facts

- ❑ Phone   678-450-7726
- ❑ Park Hours _____
- ❑ Reservations? ____Y ____N date made_____
- ❑ Open all year ____Y ____N dates_____
- ❑ Check in time _____
- ❑ Check out time _____
- ❑ Pet friendly ____Y ____N
- ❑ Max RV length _____
- ❑ Distance from home miles: _____ hours: _____
- ❑ Address_____

Fees:

- ❑ Day Use $ _____
- ❑ Camp Sites $ _____
- ❑ RV Sites $ _____
- ❑ Refund policy _____

Make It Personal

Trip dates: _____ | The weather was: Sunny Cloudy Rainy Stormy Snowy Foggy Warm Cold

Why I went:
_____

How I got there: (circle all that apply)   Plane   Train   Car   Bus   Bike   Hike   RV   MC

I went with:
_____

We stayed in (space, cabin # etc):
_____

Most relaxing day:
_____

Something funny:
_____

Someone we met:
_____

Best story told:
_____

The kids liked this:
_____

The best food:
_____

Games played:
_____

Something disappointing:
_____

Next time I'll do this differently:
_____
_____

F. D. Roosevelt State Park
City: Pine Mountain**County: Harris**

Plan your trip: https://gastateparks.org/FDRoosevelt

Activities:

- ❏ Archery
- ❏ Biking Trails
- ❏ Boating
- ❏ Canoeing
- ❏ Canyon Climbing
- ❏ Caving
- ❏ Fishing
- ❏ Geocaching
- ❏ Hiking
- ❏ Historic Sites
- ❏ Horseback
- ❏ Hunting
- ❏ Kayaking
- ❏ Nature Programs
- ❏ Photography
- ❏ Rock Climbing
- ❏ Stargazing
- ❏ Swimming
- ❏ Water Skiing
- ❏ Wildlife & Bird Watching
- ❏ Ziplining

Facilities:

- ❏ ADA
- ❏ Picnic sites
- ❏ Restrooms
- ❏ Showers
- ❏ Trailer Access
- ❏ Visitor center
- ❏ Group Camping
- ❏ RV Camp
- ❏ Rustic Camping
- ❏ Cabins / Yurts
- ❏ Day Use Area

Notes:

Get the Facts

- ❏ Phone   706-663-4858
- ❏ Park Hours _____
- ❏ Reservations? ____Y ____N date made_____
- ❏ Open all year ____Y ____N dates_____
- ❏ Check in time _____
- ❏ Check out time _____
- ❏ Pet friendly _____Y _____N
- ❏ Max RV length _____
- ❏ Distance from home miles: _____ hours: _____
- ❏ Address_____ _____ _____

Fees:

- ❏ Day Use $ _____
- ❏ Camp Sites $ _____
- ❏ RV Sites $ _____
- ❏ Refund policy _____ _____ _____

Make It Personal

Trip dates: _____ | The weather was: Sunny   Cloudy   Rainy   Stormy   Snowy   Foggy   Warm   Cold

Why I went:
_____

_____

How I got there: (circle all that apply)   Plane   Train   Car   Bus   Bike   Hike   RV   MC
_____

I went with:
_____

We stayed in (space, cabin # etc):
_____

Most relaxing day:
_____

_____

Something funny:
_____

_____

Someone we met:
_____

_____

Best story told:
_____

_____

The kids liked this:
_____

_____

The best food:
_____

_____

Games played:
_____

_____

Something disappointing:
_____

_____

Next time I'll do this differently:
_____

_____

Hartwell Lakeside Park
City: Hartwell   County: Hart

Plan your trip: https://gastateparks.org/hart

Activities:

- ❑ Archery
- ❑ Biking Trails
- ❑ Boating
- ❑ Canoeing
- ❑ Canyon Climbing
- ❑ Caving
- ❑ Fishing
- ❑ Geocaching
- ❑ Hiking
- ❑ Historic Sites
- ❑ Horseback
- ❑ Hunting
- ❑ Kayaking
- ❑ Nature Programs
- ❑ Photography
- ❑ Rock Climbing
- ❑ Stargazing
- ❑ Swimming
- ❑ Water Skiing
- ❑ Wildlife & Bird Watching
- ❑ Ziplining

Facilities:

- ❑ ADA
- ❑ Picnic sites
- ❑ Restrooms
- ❑ Showers
- ❑ Trailer Access
- ❑ Visitor center
- ❑ Group Camping
- ❑ RV Camp
- ❑ Rustic Camping
- ❑ Cabins / Yurts
- ❑ Day Use Area

Notes:

Get the Facts

- ❑ Phone   800-864-7275
- ❑ Park Hours _____
- ❑ Reservations? ____Y ____N date made_____
- ❑ Open all year ____Y ____N dates_____
- ❑ Check in time _____
- ❑ Check out time _____
- ❑ Pet friendly ____Y ____N
- ❑ Max RV length _____
- ❑ Distance from home miles: _____ hours: _____
- ❑ Address _____

Fees:

- ❑ Day Use $ _____
- ❑ Camp Sites $ _____
- ❑ RV Sites $ _____
- ❑ Refund policy _____

Make It Personal

Trip dates: _____ | The weather was: Sunny   Cloudy   Rainy   Stormy   Snowy   Foggy   Warm   Cold

Why I went:
_____

How I got there: (circle all that apply)   Plane   Train   Car   Bus   Bike   Hike   RV   MC
_____

I went with:
_____

We stayed in (space, cabin # etc):
_____

Most relaxing day:
_____

Something funny:
_____

Someone we met:
_____

Best story told:
_____

The kids liked this:
_____

The best food:
_____

Games played:
_____

Something disappointing:
_____

Next time I'll do this differently:
_____
_____

Panola Mountain State Park
City: Stockbridge   County: Henry

Plan your trip: https://gastateparks.org/PanolaMountain

Activities:

- ❏ Archery
- ❏ Biking Trails
- ❏ Boating
- ❏ Canoeing
- ❏ Canyon Climbing
- ❏ Caving
- ❏ Fishing
- ❏ Geocaching
- ❏ Hiking
- ❏ Historic Sites
- ❏ Horseback
- ❏ Hunting
- ❏ Kayaking
- ❏ Nature Programs
- ❏ Photography
- ❏ Rock Climbing
- ❏ Stargazing
- ❏ Swimming
- ❏ Water Skiing
- ❏ Wildlife & Bird Watching
- ❏ Ziplining

Facilities:

- ❏ ADA
- ❏ Picnic sites
- ❏ Restrooms
- ❏ Showers
- ❏ Trailer Access
- ❏ Visitor center
- ❏ Group Camping
- ❏ RV Camp
- ❏ Rustic Camping
- ❏ Cabins / Yurts
- ❏ Day Use Area

Notes:

Get the Facts

- ❏ Phone   770-389-7801
- ❏ Park Hours _____
- ❏ Reservations? ____Y ____N date made_____
- ❏ Open all year ____Y ____N dates_____
- ❏ Check in time _____
- ❏ Check out time _____
- ❏ Pet friendly ____Y ____N
- ❏ Max RV length _____
- ❏ Distance from home miles: _____ hours: _____
- ❏ Address_____

Fees:

- ❏ Day Use $ _____
- ❏ Camp Sites $ _____
- ❏ RV Sites $ _____
- ❏ Refund policy _____

Make It Personal

Trip dates: _____ | The weather was: Sunny   Cloudy   Rainy   Stormy   Snowy   Foggy   Warm   Cold

Why I went:
_____

_____

How I got there: (circle all that apply)   Plane   Train   Car   Bus   Bike   Hike   RV   MC
_____

I went with:
_____

We stayed in (space, cabin # etc):
_____

Most relaxing day:
_____

_____

Something funny:
_____

_____

Someone we met:
_____

_____

Best story told:
_____

_____

The kids liked this:
_____

_____

The best food:
_____

_____

Games played:
_____

_____

Something disappointing:
_____

_____

Next time I'll do this differently:
_____

_____

Elijah Clark State Park
City: Lincolnton   County: Lincoln
Plan your trip: https://gastateparks.org/ElijahClark

Activities:

- ❑ Archery
- ❑ Biking Trails
- ❑ Boating
- ❑ Canoeing
- ❑ Canyon Climbing
- ❑ Caving
- ❑ Fishing
- ❑ Geocaching
- ❑ Hiking
- ❑ Historic Sites
- ❑ Horseback
- ❑ Hunting
- ❑ Kayaking
- ❑ Nature Programs
- ❑ Photography
- ❑ Rock Climbing
- ❑ Stargazing
- ❑ Swimming
- ❑ Water Skiing
- ❑ Wildlife & Bird Watching
- ❑ Ziplining

Facilities:

- ❑ ADA
- ❑ Picnic sites
- ❑ Restrooms
- ❑ Showers
- ❑ Trailer Access
- ❑ Visitor center
- ❑ Group Camping
- ❑ RV Camp
- ❑ Rustic Camping
- ❑ Cabins / Yurts
- ❑ Day Use Area

Notes:

Get the Facts

- ❑ Phone   706-359-3458
- ❑ Park Hours _____
- ❑ Reservations? ____Y ____N
  date made_____
- ❑ Open all year ____Y ____N
  dates_____
- ❑ Check in time _____
- ❑ Check out time _____
- ❑ Pet friendly ____Y ____N
- ❑ Max RV length _____
- ❑ Distance from home
  miles: _____
  hours: _____
- ❑ Address_____
  _____
  _____

Fees:

- ❑ Day Use $ _____
- ❑ Camp Sites $ _____
- ❑ RV Sites $ _____
- ❑ Refund policy
  _____
  _____
  _____

Make It Personal

Trip dates: _____ | The weather was: Sunny   Cloudy   Rainy   Stormy   Snowy   Foggy   Warm   Cold

Why I went:
_____

How I got there: (circle all that apply)   Plane   Train   Car   Bus   Bike   Hike   RV   MC

I went with:
_____

We stayed in (space, cabin # etc):
_____

Most relaxing day:
_____

Something funny:
_____

Someone we met:
_____

Best story told:
_____

The kids liked this:
_____

The best food:
_____

Games played:
_____

Something disappointing:
_____

Next time I'll do this differently:
_____
_____

Watson Mill Bridge State Park

City: Comer **County: Madison**

Plan your trip: https://gastateparks.org/WatsonMillBridge

Activities:

- ❑ Archery
- ❑ Biking Trails
- ❑ Boating
- ❑ Canoeing
- ❑ Canyon Climbing
- ❑ Caving
- ❑ Fishing
- ❑ Geocaching
- ❑ Hiking
- ❑ Historic Sites
- ❑ Horseback
- ❑ Hunting
- ❑ Kayaking
- ❑ Nature Programs
- ❑ Photography
- ❑ Rock Climbing
- ❑ Stargazing
- ❑ Swimming
- ❑ Water Skiing
- ❑ Wildlife & Bird Watching
- ❑ Ziplining

Facilities:

- ❑ ADA
- ❑ Picnic sites
- ❑ Restrooms
- ❑ Showers
- ❑ Trailer Access
- ❑ Visitor center
- ❑ Group Camping
- ❑ RV Camp
- ❑ Rustic Camping
- ❑ Cabins / Yurts
- ❑ Day Use Area

Notes:

Get the Facts

- ❑ Phone   706-783-5349
- ❑ Park Hours _____
- ❑ Reservations? ____Y ____N date made_____
- ❑ Open all year ____Y ____N dates_____
- ❑ Check in time _____
- ❑ Check out time _____
- ❑ Pet friendly ____Y ____N
- ❑ Max RV length _____
- ❑ Distance from home
  miles: _____
  hours: _____
- ❑ Address_____

Fees:

- ❑ Day Use $ _____
- ❑ Camp Sites $ _____
- ❑ RV Sites $ _____
- ❑ Refund policy _____

Make It Personal

Trip dates: _____ | The weather was: Sunny   Cloudy   Rainy   Stormy   Snowy   Foggy   Warm   Cold

Why I went:
_____
_____

How I got there: (circle all that apply)   Plane   Train   Car   Bus   Bike   Hike   RV   MC
_____

I went with:
_____

We stayed in (space, cabin # etc):
_____

Most relaxing day:
_____
_____

Something funny:
_____
_____

Someone we met:
_____
_____

Best story told:
_____
_____

The kids liked this:
_____
_____

The best food:
_____
_____

Games played:
_____
_____

Something disappointing:
_____
_____

Next time I'll do this differently:
_____
_____

Roosevelt's Little White House State Historic Site

City: Warm Springs   **County: Meriwether**

Plan your trip: https://gastateparks.org/LittleWhiteHouse

Activities:

- ❑ Archery
- ❑ Biking Trails
- ❑ Boating
- ❑ Canoeing
- ❑ Canyon Climbing
- ❑ Caving
- ❑ Fishing
- ❑ Geocaching
- ❑ Hiking
- ❑ Historic Sites
- ❑ Horseback
- ❑ Hunting
- ❑ Kayaking
- ❑ Nature Programs
- ❑ Photography
- ❑ Rock Climbing
- ❑ Stargazing
- ❑ Swimming
- ❑ Water Skiing
- ❑ Wildlife & Bird Watching
- ❑ Ziplining
- ❑
- ❑
- ❑
- ❑
- ❑
- ❑
- ❑
- ❑
- ❑
- ❑

Facilities:

- ❑ ADA
- ❑ Picnic sites
- ❑ Restrooms
- ❑ Showers
- ❑ Trailer Access
- ❑ Visitor center
- ❑ Group Camping
- ❑ RV Camp
- ❑ Rustic Camping
- ❑ Cabins / Yurts
- ❑ Day Use Area

Notes:

Get the Facts

- ❑ Phone   706-655-5870
- ❑ Park Hours _____
- ❑ Reservations? ____Y ____N date made_____
- ❑ Open all year ____Y ____N dates_____
- ❑ Check in time _____
- ❑ Check out time _____
- ❑ Pet friendly _____Y _____N
- ❑ Max RV length _____
- ❑ Distance from home
  miles: _____
  hours: _____
- ❑ Address_____

Fees:

- ❑ Day Use $ _____
- ❑ Camp Sites $ _____
- ❑ RV Sites $ _____
- ❑ Refund policy _____

Make It Personal

Trip dates: _____ | The weather was: Sunny Cloudy Rainy Stormy Snowy Foggy Warm Cold

Why I went:
_____

How I got there: (circle all that apply)   Plane   Train   Car   Bus   Bike   Hike   RV   MC
_____

I went with:
_____

We stayed in (space, cabin # etc):
_____

Most relaxing day:
_____

Something funny:
_____

Someone we met:
_____

Best story told:
_____

The kids liked this:
_____

The best food:
_____

Games played:
_____

Something disappointing:
_____

Next time I'll do this differently:
_____
_____

High Falls State Park
City: Jackson   County: Monroe

Plan your trip: https://gastateparks.org/HighFalls

Activities:

- ❏ Archery
- ❏ Biking Trails
- ❏ Boating
- ❏ Canoeing
- ❏ Canyon Climbing
- ❏ Caving
- ❏ Fishing
- ❏ Geocaching
- ❏ Hiking
- ❏ Historic Sites
- ❏ Horseback
- ❏ Hunting
- ❏ Kayaking
- ❏ Nature Programs
- ❏ Photography
- ❏ Rock Climbing
- ❏ Stargazing
- ❏ Swimming
- ❏ Water Skiing
- ❏ Wildlife & Bird Watching
- ❏ Ziplining

Facilities:

- ❏ ADA
- ❏ Picnic sites
- ❏ Restrooms
- ❏ Showers
- ❏ Trailer Access
- ❏ Visitor center
- ❏ Group Camping
- ❏ RV Camp
- ❏ Rustic Camping
- ❏ Cabins / Yurts
- ❏ Day Use Area

Notes:

Get the Facts

- ❏ Phone   478-993-3053
- ❏ Park Hours _____
- ❏ Reservations? ____Y ____N date made_____
- ❏ Open all year ____Y ____N dates_____
- ❏ Check in time _____
- ❏ Check out time _____
- ❏ Pet friendly ____Y ____N
- ❏ Max RV length _____
- ❏ Distance from home
  miles: _____
  hours: _____
- ❏ Address_____

Fees:

- ❏ Day Use $ _____
- ❏ Camp Sites $ _____
- ❏ RV Sites $ _____
- ❏ Refund policy _____

Make It Personal

Trip dates: _____ | The weather was: Sunny   Cloudy   Rainy   Stormy   Snowy   Foggy   Warm   Cold

Why I went:
_____

How I got there: (circle all that apply)   Plane   Train   Car   Bus   Bike   Hike   RV   MC

I went with:
_____

We stayed in (space, cabin # etc):
_____

Most relaxing day:
_____

Something funny:
_____

Someone we met:
_____

Best story told:
_____

The kids liked this:
_____

The best food:
_____

Games played:
_____

Something disappointing:
_____

Next time I'll do this differently:
_____

Hard Labor Creek State Park

City: Rutledge **County: Morgan**

Plan your trip: https://gastateparks.org/HardLaborCreek

Activities:

- ❑ Archery
- ❑ Biking Trails
- ❑ Boating
- ❑ Canoeing
- ❑ Canyon Climbing
- ❑ Caving
- ❑ Fishing
- ❑ Geocaching
- ❑ Hiking
- ❑ Historic Sites
- ❑ Horseback
- ❑ Hunting
- ❑ Kayaking
- ❑ Nature Programs
- ❑ Photography
- ❑ Rock Climbing
- ❑ Stargazing
- ❑ Swimming
- ❑ Water Skiing
- ❑ Wildlife & Bird Watching
- ❑ Ziplining

Facilities:

- ❑ ADA
- ❑ Picnic sites
- ❑ Restrooms
- ❑ Showers
- ❑ Trailer Access
- ❑ Visitor center
- ❑ Group Camping
- ❑ RV Camp
- ❑ Rustic Camping
- ❑ Cabins / Yurts
- ❑ Day Use Area

Notes:

Get the Facts

- ❑ Phone   706-557-3001
- ❑ Park Hours _____
- ❑ Reservations? ____Y ____N date made_____
- ❑ Open all year ____Y ____N dates_____
- ❑ Check in time _____
- ❑ Check out time _____
- ❑ Pet friendly ____Y ____N
- ❑ Max RV length _____
- ❑ Distance from home miles: _____ hours: _____
- ❑ Address _____

Fees:

- ❑ Day Use $ _____
- ❑ Camp Sites $ _____
- ❑ RV Sites $ _____
- ❑ Refund policy _____

Make It Personal

Trip dates: _____ | The weather was: Sunny Cloudy Rainy Stormy Snowy Foggy Warm Cold

Why I went:
_____
_____

How I got there: (circle all that apply)   Plane   Train   Car   Bus   Bike   Hike   RV   MC
_____

I went with:
_____

We stayed in (space, cabin # etc):
_____

Most relaxing day:
_____
_____

Something funny:
_____
_____

Someone we met:
_____
_____

Best story told:
_____
_____

The kids liked this:
_____
_____

The best food:
_____
_____

Games played:
_____
_____

Something disappointing:
_____
_____

Next time I'll do this differently:
_____
_____

A.H. Stephens State Park
City: Crawfordville   County: Taliaferro

Plan your trip: https://gastateparks.org/AHStephens

Activities:

- ☐ Archery
- ☐ Biking Trails
- ☐ Boating
- ☐ Canoeing
- ☐ Canyon Climbing
- ☐ Caving
- ☐ Fishing
- ☐ Geocaching
- ☐ Hiking
- ☐ Historic Sites
- ☐ Horseback
- ☐ Hunting
- ☐ Kayaking
- ☐ Nature Programs
- ☐ Photography
- ☐ Rock Climbing
- ☐ Stargazing
- ☐ Swimming
- ☐ Water Skiing
- ☐ Wildlife & Bird Watching
- ☐ Ziplining

Facilities:

- ☐ ADA
- ☐ Picnic sites
- ☐ Restrooms
- ☐ Showers
- ☐ Trailer Access
- ☐ Visitor center
- ☐ Group Camping
- ☐ RV Camp
- ☐ Rustic Camping
- ☐ Cabins / Yurts
- ☐ Day Use Area

Notes:

Get the Facts

- ☐ Phone   706-456-2602
- ☐ Park Hours _____
- ☐ Reservations? ____Y ____N date made_____
- ☐ Open all year ____Y ____N dates_____
- ☐ Check in time _____
- ☐ Check out time _____
- ☐ Pet friendly ____Y ____N
- ☐ Max RV length _____
- ☐ Distance from home
  miles: _____
  hours: _____
- ☐ Address_____

Fees:

- ☐ Day Use $ _____
- ☐ Camp Sites $ _____
- ☐ RV Sites $ _____
- ☐ Refund policy _____

Make It Personal

Trip dates: _____ | The weather was: Sunny Cloudy Rainy Stormy Snowy Foggy Warm Cold

Why I went:
_____
_____

How I got there: (circle all that apply)   Plane   Train   Car   Bus   Bike   Hike   RV   MC
_____

I went with:
_____

We stayed in (space, cabin # etc):
_____

Most relaxing day:
_____
_____

Something funny:
_____
_____

Someone we met:
_____
_____

Best story told:
_____
_____

The kids liked this:
_____
_____

The best food:
_____
_____

Games played:
_____
_____

Something disappointing:
_____
_____

Next time I'll do this differently:
_____
_____

Hamburg State Park
City: Mitchell   County: Warren
Plan your trip: https://gastateparks.org/Hamburg

Activities:

- ❏ Archery
- ❏ Biking Trails
- ❏ Boating
- ❏ Canoeing
- ❏ Canyon Climbing
- ❏ Caving
- ❏ Fishing
- ❏ Geocaching
- ❏ Hiking
- ❏ Historic Sites
- ❏ Horseback
- ❏ Hunting
- ❏ Kayaking
- ❏ Nature Programs
- ❏ Photography
- ❏ Rock Climbing
- ❏ Stargazing
- ❏ Swimming
- ❏ Water Skiing
- ❏ Wildlife & Bird Watching
- ❏ Ziplining

Facilities:

- ❏ ADA
- ❏ Picnic sites
- ❏ Restrooms
- ❏ Showers
- ❏ Trailer Access
- ❏ Visitor center
- ❏ Group Camping
- ❏ RV Camp
- ❏ Rustic Camping
- ❏ Cabins / Yurts
- ❏ Day Use Area

Notes:

Get the Facts

- ❏ Phone   478-552-2393
- ❏ Park Hours _____
- ❏ Reservations? ____Y ____N date made_____
- ❏ Open all year ____Y ____N dates_____
- ❏ Check in time _____
- ❏ Check out time _____
- ❏ Pet friendly ____Y ____N
- ❏ Max RV length _____
- ❏ Distance from home
  miles: _____
  hours: _____
- ❏ Address_____

Fees:

- ❏ Day Use $ _____
- ❏ Camp Sites $ _____
- ❏ RV Sites $ _____
- ❏ Refund policy _____

Make It Personal

Trip dates: _____ | The weather was: Sunny   Cloudy   Rainy   Stormy   Snowy   Foggy   Warm   Cold

Why I went:
_____

How I got there: (circle all that apply)   Plane   Train   Car   Bus   Bike   Hike   RV   MC

I went with: _____

We stayed in (space, cabin # etc): _____

Most relaxing day:
_____

Something funny:
_____

Someone we met:
_____

Best story told:
_____

The kids liked this:
_____

The best food:
_____

Games played:
_____

Something disappointing:
_____

Next time I'll do this differently:
_____

Jarrell Plantation State Historic Site

City: Juliette **County: Monroe**

Plan your trip: https://gastateparks.org/JarrellPlantation

Activities:

- ❑ Bike Trails ❑
- ❑ Bird Watching ❑
- ❑ Boating ❑
- ❑ Fishing ❑
- ❑ Hiking ❑
- ❑ Historic Site ❑
- ❑ Hunting ❑
- ❑ Geocaching ❑
- ❑ Nature Trails ❑
- ❑ Watersports ❑
- ❑ Wildlife Viewing ❑

Facilities:

- ❑ ADA ❑
- ❑ Gift Shop ❑
- ❑ Museum ❑
- ❑ Visitor Center ❑
- ❑ Picnic sites ❑
- ❑ Restrooms ❑

Things to do in the area:

Get the Facts

- ❑ Phone 478-986-5172
- ❑ Park Hours _____
- ❑ Reservations? ____Y ____N date made_____
- ❑ Open all year? ____Y____N dates_____
- ❑ Dog friendly ____Y ____N
- ❑ Distance from home
  miles: _____
  hours: _____
- ❑ Address_____
  _____
  _____

Fees:

- ❑ Day Use $ _____
- ❑ Refund policy
  _____
  _____
  _____

Notes:

78

Traveler's Rest State Historic Site

City: Toccoa   **County: Stephens**

Plan your trip: https://gastateparks.org/TravelersRest

Activities:

- ❏ Bike Trails
- ❏ Bird Watching
- ❏ Boating
- ❏ Fishing
- ❏ Hiking
- ❏ Historic Site
- ❏ Hunting
- ❏ Geocaching
- ❏ Nature Trails
- ❏ Watersports
- ❏ Wildlife Viewing

Facilities:

- ❏ ADA
- ❏ Gift Shop
- ❏ Museum
- ❏ Visitor Center
- ❏ Picnic sites
- ❏ Restrooms

Things to do in the area:

Get the Facts

- ❏ Phone 706-886-2256
- ❏ Park Hours _____
- ❏ Reservations? ____Y ____N
  date made_____
- ❏ Open all year? ____Y____N
  dates_____
- ❏ Dog friendly ____Y ____N
- ❏ Distance from home
  miles: _____
  hours: _____
- ❏ Address_____
  _____
  _____

Fees:

- ❏ Day Use $ _____
- ❏ Refund policy
  _____
  _____
  _____

Notes:

Robert Toombs House State Historic Site
City: Washington   County: Wilkes

Plan your trip: https://gastateparks.org/RobertToombsHouse

Activities:

- ❑ Bike Trails ❑
- ❑ Bird Watching ❑
- ❑ Boating ❑
- ❑ Fishing ❑
- ❑ Hiking ❑
- ❑ Historic Site ❑
- ❑ Hunting ❑
- ❑ Geocaching ❑
- ❑ Nature Trails ❑
- ❑ Watersports ❑
- ❑ Wildlife Viewing ❑

Facilities:

- ❑ ADA ❑
- ❑ Gift Shop ❑
- ❑ Museum ❑
- ❑ Visitor Center ❑
- ❑ Picnic sites ❑
- ❑ Restrooms ❑

Things to do in the area:

Get the Facts

- ❑ Phone 706-678-2226
- ❑ Park Hours _____
- ❑ Reservations? ____Y ____N date made_____
- ❑ Open all year? ____Y ____N dates_____
- ❑ Dog friendly ____Y ____N
- ❑ Distance from home
  miles: _____
  hours: _____
- ❑ Address_____

Fees:

- ❑ Day Use $ _____
- ❑ Refund policy _____

Notes:

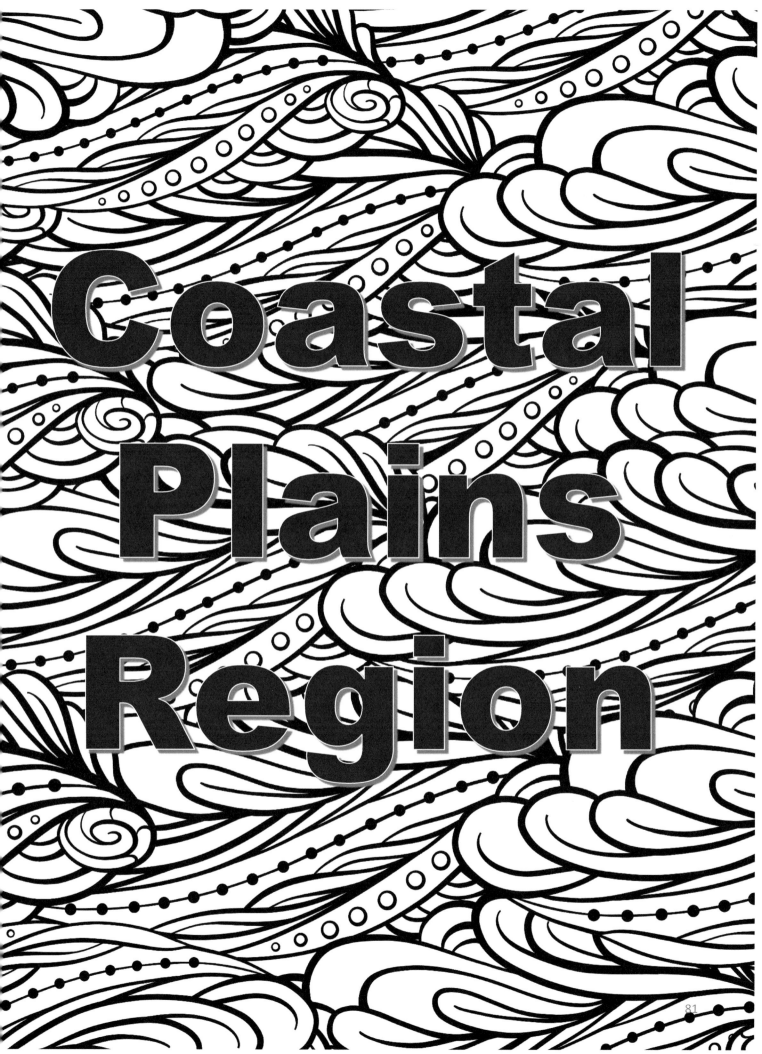

George T. Bagby State Park
City: Fort Gaines   County: Clay

Plan your trip: http://www.georgetbagbylodge.com/

Activities:

- ❏ Archery
- ❏ Biking Trails
- ❏ Boating
- ❏ Canoeing
- ❏ Canyon Climbing
- ❏ Caving
- ❏ Fishing
- ❏ Geocaching
- ❏ Hiking
- ❏ Historic Sites
- ❏ Horseback
- ❏ Hunting
- ❏ Kayaking
- ❏ Nature Programs
- ❏ Photography
- ❏ Rock Climbing
- ❏ Stargazing
- ❏ Swimming
- ❏ Water Skiing
- ❏ Wildlife & Bird Watching
- ❏ Ziplining
- ❏
- ❏
- ❏
- ❏
- ❏
- ❏
- ❏
- ❏
- ❏
- ❏

Facilities:

- ❏ ADA
- ❏ Picnic sites
- ❏ Restrooms
- ❏ Showers
- ❏ Trailer Access
- ❏ Visitor center
- ❏ Group Camping
- ❏ RV Camp
- ❏ Rustic Camping
- ❏ Cabins / Yurts
- ❏ Day Use Area

Notes:

Get the Facts

- ❏ Phone   229-768-2571
- ❏ Park Hours _____
- ❏ Reservations? ____Y ____N
  date made_____
- ❏ Open all year ____Y ____N
  dates_____
- ❏ Check in time _____
- ❏ Check out time _____
- ❏ Pet friendly _____Y _____N
- ❏ Max RV length _____
- ❏ Distance from home
  miles: _____
  hours: _____
- ❏ Address_____
  _____
  _____

Fees:

- ❏ Day Use $ _____
- ❏ Camp Sites $ _____
- ❏ RV Sites $ _____
- ❏ Refund policy _____
  _____
  _____

Make It Personal

Trip dates: _____ | The weather was: Sunny   Cloudy   Rainy   Stormy   Snowy   Foggy   Warm   Cold

Why I went:
_____

How I got there: (circle all that apply)   Plane   Train   Car   Bus   Bike   Hike   RV   MC

I went with:
_____

We stayed in (space, cabin # etc):
_____

Most relaxing day:
_____

Something funny:
_____

Someone we met:
_____

Best story told:
_____

The kids liked this:
_____

The best food:
_____

Games played:
_____

Something disappointing:
_____

Next time I'll do this differently:
_____
_____

General Coffee State Park

City: Nicholls **County: Coffee**

Plan your trip: https://gastateparks.org/GeneralCoffee

Activities:

- ❏ Archery
- ❏ Biking Trails
- ❏ Boating
- ❏ Canoeing
- ❏ Canyon Climbing
- ❏ Caving
- ❏ Fishing
- ❏ Geocaching
- ❏ Hiking
- ❏ Historic Sites
- ❏ Horseback
- ❏ Hunting
- ❏ Kayaking
- ❏ Nature Programs
- ❏ Photography
- ❏ Rock Climbing
- ❏ Stargazing
- ❏ Swimming
- ❏ Water Skiing
- ❏ Wildlife & Bird Watching
- ❏ Ziplining
- ❏
- ❏
- ❏
- ❏
- ❏
- ❏
- ❏
- ❏
- ❏
- ❏
- ❏

Facilities:

- ❏ ADA
- ❏ Picnic sites
- ❏ Restrooms
- ❏ Showers
- ❏ Trailer Access
- ❏ Visitor center
- ❏ Group Camping
- ❏ RV Camp
- ❏ Rustic Camping
- ❏ Cabins / Yurts
- ❏ Day Use Area

Notes:

Get the Facts

- ❏ Phone   912-384-7082
- ❏ Park Hours _____
- ❏ Reservations? ____Y ____N date made_____
- ❏ Open all year ____Y ____N dates_____
- ❏ Check in time _____
- ❏ Check out time _____
- ❏ Pet friendly ____Y ____N
- ❏ Max RV length _____
- ❏ Distance from home miles: _____ hours: _____
- ❏ Address_____

Fees:

- ❏ Day Use $ _____
- ❏ Camp Sites $ _____
- ❏ RV Sites $ _____
- ❏ Refund policy _____

Make It Personal

Trip dates: _____ | The weather was: Sunny   Cloudy   Rainy   Stormy   Snowy   Foggy   Warm   Cold

Why I went:
_____
_____

How I got there: (circle all that apply)   Plane   Train   Car   Bus   Bike   Hike   RV   MC
_____

I went with:
_____

We stayed in (space, cabin # etc):
_____

Most relaxing day:
_____
_____

Something funny:
_____
_____

Someone we met:
_____
_____

Best story told:
_____
_____

The kids liked this:
_____
_____

The best food:
_____
_____

Games played:
_____
_____

Something disappointing:
_____
_____

Next time I'll do this differently:
_____
_____

Reed Bingham State Park

City: Adel　　　　　　　　**County: Colquitt**

Plan your trip: https://gastateparks.org/ReedBingham

Activities:

- ❑ Archery
- ❑ Biking Trails
- ❑ Boating
- ❑ Canoeing
- ❑ Canyon Climbing
- ❑ Caving
- ❑ Fishing
- ❑ Geocaching
- ❑ Hiking
- ❑ Historic Sites
- ❑ Horseback
- ❑ Hunting
- ❑ Kayaking
- ❑ Nature Programs
- ❑ Photography
- ❑ Rock Climbing
- ❑ Stargazing
- ❑ Swimming
- ❑ Water Skiing
- ❑ Wildlife & Bird Watching
- ❑ Ziplining

Facilities:

- ❑ ADA
- ❑ Picnic sites
- ❑ Restrooms
- ❑ Showers
- ❑ Trailer Access
- ❑ Visitor center
- ❑ Group Camping
- ❑ RV Camp
- ❑ Rustic Camping
- ❑ Cabins / Yurts
- ❑ Day Use Area

Notes:

Get the Facts

- ❑ Phone   229-896-3551
- ❑ Park Hours _____
- ❑ Reservations? ____Y ____N date made_____
- ❑ Open all year ____Y ____N dates_____
- ❑ Check in time _____
- ❑ Check out time _____
- ❑ Pet friendly ____Y ____N
- ❑ Max RV length _____
- ❑ Distance from home
  miles: _____
  hours: _____
- ❑ Address_____

Fees:

- ❑ Day Use $ _____
- ❑ Camp Sites $ _____
- ❑ RV Sites $ _____
- ❑ Refund policy _____

Make It Personal

Trip dates: _____ | The weather was: Sunny Cloudy Rainy Stormy Snowy Foggy Warm Cold

Why I went:
_____

_____

How I got there: (circle all that apply)   Plane   Train   Car   Bus   Bike   Hike   RV   MC
_____

I went with:
_____

We stayed in (space, cabin # etc):
_____

Most relaxing day:
_____

_____

Something funny:
_____

_____

Someone we met:
_____

_____

Best story told:
_____

_____

The kids liked this:
_____

_____

The best food:
_____

_____

Games played:
_____

_____

Something disappointing:
_____

_____

Next time I'll do this differently:
_____

_____

Georgia Veterans State Park
City: Cordele   County: Crisp

Plan your trip: https://www.lakeblackshearresort.com/

Activities:

- ❑ Archery
- ❑ Biking Trails
- ❑ Boating
- ❑ Canoeing
- ❑ Canyon Climbing
- ❑ Caving
- ❑ Fishing
- ❑ Geocaching
- ❑ Hiking
- ❑ Historic Sites
- ❑ Horseback
- ❑ Hunting
- ❑ Kayaking
- ❑ Nature Programs
- ❑ Photography
- ❑ Rock Climbing
- ❑ Stargazing
- ❑ Swimming
- ❑ Water Skiing
- ❑ Wildlife & Bird Watching
- ❑ Ziplining

Facilities:

- ❑ ADA
- ❑ Picnic sites
- ❑ Restrooms
- ❑ Showers
- ❑ Trailer Access
- ❑ Visitor center
- ❑ Group Camping
- ❑ RV Camp
- ❑ Rustic Camping
- ❑ Cabins / Yurts
- ❑ Day Use Area

Notes:

Get the Facts

- ❑ Phone   800-459-1230
- ❑ Park Hours _____
- ❑ Reservations? ____Y ____N date made_____
- ❑ Open all year ____Y ____N dates_____
- ❑ Check in time _____
- ❑ Check out time _____
- ❑ Pet friendly _____Y _____N
- ❑ Max RV length _____
- ❑ Distance from home
  miles: _____
  hours: _____
- ❑ Address _____

Fees:

- ❑ Day Use $ _____
- ❑ Camp Sites $ _____
- ❑ RV Sites $ _____
- ❑ Refund policy _____

Make It Personal

Trip dates: _____ | The weather was: Sunny   Cloudy   Rainy   Stormy   Snowy   Foggy   Warm   Cold

Why I went:
_____

_____

How I got there: (circle all that apply)   Plane   Train   Car   Bus   Bike   Hike   RV   MC
_____

I went with:
_____

We stayed in (space, cabin # etc):
_____

Most relaxing day:
_____

_____

Something funny:
_____

_____

Someone we met:
_____

_____

Best story told:
_____

_____

The kids liked this:
_____

_____

The best food:
_____

_____

Games played:
_____

_____

Something disappointing:
_____

_____

Next time I'll do this differently:
_____

_____

Kolomoki Mounds State Park

City: Blakely **County: Early**

Plan your trip: https://gastateparks.org/KolomokiMounds

Activities:

- ❑ Archery
- ❑ Biking Trails
- ❑ Boating
- ❑ Canoeing
- ❑ Canyon Climbing
- ❑ Caving
- ❑ Fishing
- ❑ Geocaching
- ❑ Hiking
- ❑ Historic Sites
- ❑ Horseback
- ❑ Hunting
- ❑ Kayaking
- ❑ Nature Programs
- ❑ Photography
- ❑ Rock Climbing
- ❑ Stargazing
- ❑ Swimming
- ❑ Water Skiing
- ❑ Wildlife & Bird Watching
- ❑ Ziplining

Facilities:

- ❑ ADA
- ❑ Picnic sites
- ❑ Restrooms
- ❑ Showers
- ❑ Trailer Access
- ❑ Visitor center
- ❑ Group Camping
- ❑ RV Camp
- ❑ Rustic Camping
- ❑ Cabins / Yurts
- ❑ Day Use Area

Notes:

Get the Facts

- ❑ Phone   229-724-2150
- ❑ Park Hours _____
- ❑ Reservations? ____Y ____N date made_____
- ❑ Open all year ____Y ____N dates_____
- ❑ Check in time _____
- ❑ Check out time _____
- ❑ Pet friendly ____Y ____N
- ❑ Max RV length _____
- ❑ Distance from home
  miles: _____
  hours: _____
- ❑ Address_____

Fees:

- ❑ Day Use $ _____
- ❑ Camp Sites $ _____
- ❑ RV Sites $ _____
- ❑ Refund policy _____

Make It Personal

Trip dates: _____ | The weather was: Sunny   Cloudy   Rainy   Stormy   Snowy   Foggy   Warm   Cold

Why I went:
_____
_____

How I got there: (circle all that apply)   Plane   Train   Car   Bus   Bike   Hike   RV   MC

I went with:
_____

We stayed in (space, cabin # etc):
_____

Most relaxing day:
_____
_____

Something funny:
_____
_____

Someone we met:
_____
_____

Best story told:
_____
_____

The kids liked this:
_____
_____

The best food:
_____
_____

Games played:
_____
_____

Something disappointing:
_____
_____

Next time I'll do this differently:
_____
_____

George L. Smith State Park

City: Twin **County: Emanuel**

Plan your trip: https://gastateparks.org/GeorgeLSmith

Activities:

- ❏ Archery
- ❏ Biking Trails
- ❏ Boating
- ❏ Canoeing
- ❏ Canyon Climbing
- ❏ Caving
- ❏ Fishing
- ❏ Geocaching
- ❏ Hiking
- ❏ Historic Sites
- ❏ Horseback
- ❏ Hunting
- ❏ Kayaking
- ❏ Nature Programs
- ❏ Photography
- ❏ Rock Climbing
- ❏ Stargazing
- ❏ Swimming
- ❏ Water Skiing
- ❏ Wildlife & Bird Watching
- ❏ Ziplining

Facilities:

- ❏ ADA
- ❏ Picnic sites
- ❏ Restrooms
- ❏ Showers
- ❏ Trailer Access
- ❏ Visitor center
- ❏ Group Camping
- ❏ RV Camp
- ❏ Rustic Camping
- ❏ Cabins / Yurts
- ❏ Day Use Area

Notes:

Get the Facts

- ❏ Phone   478-763-2759
- ❏ Park Hours _____
- ❏ Reservations? ____Y ____N date made_____
- ❏ Open all year ____Y ____N dates_____
- ❏ Check in time _____
- ❏ Check out time _____
- ❏ Pet friendly ____Y ____N
- ❏ Max RV length _____
- ❏ Distance from home
  miles: _____
  hours: _____
- ❏ Address_____

Fees:

- ❏ Day Use $ _____
- ❏ Camp Sites $ _____
- ❏ RV Sites $ _____
- ❏ Refund policy _____

Make It Personal

Trip dates: _____ | The weather was: Sunny   Cloudy   Rainy   Stormy   Snowy   Foggy   Warm   Cold

Why I went: _____

_____

How I got there: (circle all that apply)   Plane   Train   Car   Bus   Bike   Hike   RV   MC

I went with: _____

We stayed in (space, cabin # etc): _____

Most relaxing day: _____

_____

Something funny: _____

_____

Someone we met: _____

_____

Best story told: _____

_____

The kids liked this: _____

_____

The best food: _____

_____

Games played: _____

_____

Something disappointing: _____

_____

Next time I'll do this differently: _____

_____

Magnolia Springs State Park

City: Millen **County: Jenkins**

Plan your trip: https://gastateparks.org/MagnoliaSprings

Activities:

- ❑ Archery
- ❑ Biking Trails
- ❑ Boating
- ❑ Canoeing
- ❑ Canyon Climbing
- ❑ Caving
- ❑ Fishing
- ❑ Geocaching
- ❑ Hiking
- ❑ Historic Sites
- ❑ Horseback
- ❑ Hunting
- ❑ Kayaking
- ❑ Nature Programs
- ❑ Photography
- ❑ Rock Climbing
- ❑ Stargazing
- ❑ Swimming
- ❑ Water Skiing
- ❑ Wildlife & Bird Watching
- ❑ Ziplining

Facilities:

- ❑ ADA
- ❑ Picnic sites
- ❑ Restrooms
- ❑ Showers
- ❑ Trailer Access
- ❑ Visitor center
- ❑ Group Camping
- ❑ RV Camp
- ❑ Rustic Camping
- ❑ Cabins / Yurts
- ❑ Day Use Area

Notes:

Get the Facts

- ❑ Phone   478-982-1660
- ❑ Park Hours _____
- ❑ Reservations? ____Y ____N date made_____
- ❑ Open all year ____Y ____N dates_____
- ❑ Check in time _____
- ❑ Check out time _____
- ❑ Pet friendly ____Y ____N
- ❑ Max RV length _____
- ❑ Distance from home
  miles: _____
  hours: _____
- ❑ Address_____

Fees:

- ❑ Day Use $ _____
- ❑ Camp Sites $ _____
- ❑ RV Sites $ _____
- ❑ Refund policy _____

Make It Personal

Trip dates: _____ | The weather was: Sunny Cloudy Rainy Stormy Snowy Foggy Warm Cold

Why I went:
_____

_____

How I got there: (circle all that apply)   Plane   Train   Car   Bus   Bike   Hike   RV   MC
_____

I went with:
_____

We stayed in (space, cabin # etc):
_____

Most relaxing day:
_____

_____

Something funny:
_____

_____

Someone we met:
_____

_____

Best story told:
_____

_____

The kids liked this:
_____

_____

The best food:
_____

_____

Games played:
_____

_____

Something disappointing:
_____

_____

Next time I'll do this differently:
_____

_____

Seminole State Park
City: Donalsonville   County: Seminole
Plan your trip: https://gastateparks.org/Seminole

Activities:

- ❑ Archery
- ❑ Biking Trails
- ❑ Boating
- ❑ Canoeing
- ❑ Canyon Climbing
- ❑ Caving
- ❑ Fishing
- ❑ Geocaching
- ❑ Hiking
- ❑ Historic Sites
- ❑ Horseback
- ❑ Hunting
- ❑ Kayaking
- ❑ Nature Programs
- ❑ Photography
- ❑ Rock Climbing
- ❑ Stargazing
- ❑ Swimming
- ❑ Water Skiing
- ❑ Wildlife & Bird Watching
- ❑ Ziplining

Facilities:

- ❑ ADA
- ❑ Picnic sites
- ❑ Restrooms
- ❑ Showers
- ❑ Trailer Access
- ❑ Visitor center
- ❑ Group Camping
- ❑ RV Camp
- ❑ Rustic Camping
- ❑ Cabins / Yurts
- ❑ Day Use Area

Notes:

Get the Facts

- ❑ Phone   229-861-3137
- ❑ Park Hours _____
- ❑ Reservations? ____Y ____N date made_____
- ❑ Open all year ____Y ____N dates_____
- ❑ Check in time _____
- ❑ Check out time _____
- ❑ Pet friendly ____Y ____N
- ❑ Max RV length _____
- ❑ Distance from home
  miles: _____
  hours: _____
- ❑ Address_____

Fees:

- ❑ Day Use $ _____
- ❑ Camp Sites $ _____
- ❑ RV Sites $ _____
- ❑ Refund policy _____

Make It Personal

Trip dates: _____ | The weather was: Sunny   Cloudy   Rainy   Stormy   Snowy   Foggy   Warm   Cold
_____

Why I went:
_____

_____

How I got there: (circle all that apply)   Plane   Train   Car   Bus   Bike   Hike   RV   MC
_____

I went with:
_____

We stayed in (space, cabin # etc):
_____

Most relaxing day:
_____

_____

Something funny:
_____

_____

Someone we met:
_____

_____

Best story told:
_____

_____

The kids liked this:
_____

_____

The best food:
_____

_____

Games played:
_____

_____

Something disappointing:
_____

_____

Next time I'll do this differently:
_____

_____

Providence Canyon State Outdoor Recreation Area

City: Lumpkin   **County: Stewart**

Plan your trip: https://gastateparks.org/ProvidenceCanyon

Activities:

- ❑ Archery
- ❑ Biking Trails
- ❑ Boating
- ❑ Canoeing
- ❑ Canyon Climbing
- ❑ Caving
- ❑ Fishing
- ❑ Geocaching
- ❑ Hiking
- ❑ Historic Sites
- ❑ Horseback
- ❑ Hunting
- ❑ Kayaking
- ❑ Nature Programs
- ❑ Photography
- ❑ Rock Climbing
- ❑ Stargazing
- ❑ Swimming
- ❑ Water Skiing
- ❑ Wildlife & Bird Watching
- ❑ Ziplining

Facilities:

- ❑ ADA
- ❑ Picnic sites
- ❑ Restrooms
- ❑ Showers
- ❑ Trailer Access
- ❑ Visitor center
- ❑ Group Camping
- ❑ RV Camp
- ❑ Rustic Camping
- ❑ Cabins / Yurts
- ❑ Day Use Area

Notes:

Get the Facts

- ❑ Phone   229-838-6202
- ❑ Park Hours _____
- ❑ Reservations? ____Y ____N date made_____
- ❑ Open all year ____Y ____N dates_____
- ❑ Check in time _____
- ❑ Check out time _____
- ❑ Pet friendly _____Y _____N
- ❑ Max RV length _____
- ❑ Distance from home
  miles: _____
  hours: _____
- ❑ Address_____

Fees:

- ❑ Day Use $ _____
- ❑ Camp Sites $ _____
- ❑ RV Sites $ _____
- ❑ Refund policy _____

Make It Personal

Trip dates: _____ | The weather was: Sunny   Cloudy   Rainy   Stormy   Snowy   Foggy   Warm   Cold

Why I went:
_____
_____

How I got there: (circle all that apply)   Plane   Train   Car   Bus   Bike   Hike   RV   MC
_____

I went with:
_____

We stayed in (space, cabin # etc):
_____

Most relaxing day:
_____
_____

Something funny:
_____
_____

Someone we met:
_____
_____

Best story told:
_____
_____

The kids liked this:
_____
_____

The best food:
_____
_____

Games played:
_____
_____

Something disappointing:
_____
_____

Next time I'll do this differently:
_____
_____

Florence Marina State Park
City: Omaha   County: Stewart

Plan your trip: https://gastateparks.org/FlorenceMarina

Activities:

- ❑ Archery
- ❑ Biking Trails
- ❑ Boating
- ❑ Canoeing
- ❑ Canyon Climbing
- ❑ Caving
- ❑ Fishing
- ❑ Geocaching
- ❑ Hiking
- ❑ Historic Sites
- ❑ Horseback
- ❑ Hunting
- ❑ Kayaking
- ❑ Nature Programs
- ❑ Photography
- ❑ Rock Climbing
- ❑ Stargazing
- ❑ Swimming
- ❑ Water Skiing
- ❑ Wildlife & Bird Watching
- ❑ Ziplining

Facilities:

- ❑ ADA
- ❑ Picnic sites
- ❑ Restrooms
- ❑ Showers
- ❑ Trailer Access
- ❑ Visitor center
- ❑ Group Camping
- ❑ RV Camp
- ❑ Rustic Camping
- ❑ Cabins / Yurts
- ❑ Day Use Area

Notes:

Get the Facts

- ❑ Phone   229-838-6870
- ❑ Park Hours _____
- ❑ Reservations? ____Y ____N date made_____
- ❑ Open all year ____Y ____N dates_____
- ❑ Check in time _____
- ❑ Check out time _____
- ❑ Pet friendly _____Y _____N
- ❑ Max RV length _____
- ❑ Distance from home
  miles: _____
  hours: _____
- ❑ Address_____

Fees:

- ❑ Day Use $ _____
- ❑ Camp Sites $ _____
- ❑ RV Sites $ _____
- ❑ Refund policy _____

Make It Personal

Trip dates: | The weather was: Sunny   Cloudy   Rainy   Stormy   Snowy   Foggy   Warm   Cold

Why I went:

How I got there: (circle all that apply)   Plane   Train   Car   Bus   Bike   Hike   RV   MC

I went with:

We stayed in (space, cabin # etc):

Most relaxing day:

Something funny:

Someone we met:

Best story told:

The kids liked this:

The best food:

Games played:

Something disappointing:

Next time I'll do this differently:

Jack Hill State Park
City: Reidsville   County: Tattnall

Plan your trip: https://gastateparks.org/JackHill

Activities:

- ❏ Archery
- ❏ Biking Trails
- ❏ Boating
- ❏ Canoeing
- ❏ Canyon Climbing
- ❏ Caving
- ❏ Fishing
- ❏ Geocaching
- ❏ Hiking
- ❏ Historic Sites
- ❏ Horseback
- ❏ Hunting
- ❏ Kayaking
- ❏ Nature Programs
- ❏ Photography
- ❏ Rock Climbing
- ❏ Stargazing
- ❏ Swimming
- ❏ Water Skiing
- ❏ Wildlife & Bird Watching
- ❏ Ziplining

Facilities:

- ❏ ADA
- ❏ Picnic sites
- ❏ Restrooms
- ❏ Showers
- ❏ Trailer Access
- ❏ Visitor center
- ❏ Group Camping
- ❏ RV Camp
- ❏ Rustic Camping
- ❏ Cabins / Yurts
- ❏ Day Use Area

Notes:

Get the Facts

- ❏ Phone   912-557-7744
- ❏ Park Hours _____
- ❏ Reservations? ____Y ____N   date made_____
- ❏ Open all year ____Y ____N   dates_____
- ❏ Check in time _____
- ❏ Check out time _____
- ❏ Pet friendly ____Y ____N
- ❏ Max RV length _____
- ❏ Distance from home
  miles: _____
  hours: _____
- ❏ Address_____

Fees:

- ❏ Day Use $ _____
- ❏ Camp Sites $ _____
- ❏ RV Sites $ _____
- ❏ Refund policy _____

Make It Personal

Trip dates: _____ | The weather was: Sunny Cloudy Rainy Stormy Snowy Foggy Warm Cold

Why I went:
_____

_____

How I got there: (circle all that apply)   Plane   Train   Car   Bus   Bike   Hike   RV   MC
_____

I went with:
_____

We stayed in (space, cabin # etc):
_____

Most relaxing day:
_____

_____

Something funny:
_____

_____

Someone we met:
_____

_____

Best story told:
_____

_____

The kids liked this:
_____

_____

The best food:
_____

_____

Games played:
_____

_____

Something disappointing:
_____

_____

Next time I'll do this differently:
_____

_____

Little Ocmulgee State Park & Lodge

City: Helena **County: Telfair**

Plan your trip: https://www.littleocmulgeelodge.com/

Activities:

- ❑ Archery
- ❑ Biking Trails
- ❑ Boating
- ❑ Canoeing
- ❑ Canyon Climbing
- ❑ Caving
- ❑ Fishing
- ❑ Geocaching
- ❑ Hiking
- ❑ Historic Sites
- ❑ Horseback
- ❑ Hunting
- ❑ Kayaking
- ❑ Nature Programs
- ❑ Photography
- ❑ Rock Climbing
- ❑ Stargazing
- ❑ Swimming
- ❑ Water Skiing
- ❑ Wildlife & Bird Watching
- ❑ Ziplining
- ❑
- ❑
- ❑
- ❑
- ❑
- ❑
- ❑
- ❑
- ❑
- ❑
- ❑

Facilities:

- ❑ ADA
- ❑ Picnic sites
- ❑ Restrooms
- ❑ Showers
- ❑ Trailer Access
- ❑ Visitor center
- ❑ Group Camping
- ❑ RV Camp
- ❑ Rustic Camping
- ❑ Cabins / Yurts
- ❑ Day Use Area

Notes:

Get the Facts

- ❑ Phone 877-591-5572
- ❑ Park Hours _____
- ❑ Reservations? ____Y ____N date made_____
- ❑ Open all year ____Y ____N dates_____
- ❑ Check in time _____
- ❑ Check out time _____
- ❑ Pet friendly _____Y _____N
- ❑ Max RV length _____
- ❑ Distance from home miles: _____ hours: _____
- ❑ Address_____

Fees:

- ❑ Day Use $ _____
- ❑ Camp Sites $ _____
- ❑ RV Sites $ _____
- ❑ Refund policy _____

Make It Personal

Trip dates: _____ | The weather was: Sunny   Cloudy   Rainy   Stormy   Snowy   Foggy   Warm   Cold

Why I went: _____

_____

How I got there: (circle all that apply)   Plane   Train   Car   Bus   Bike   Hike   RV   MC

I went with: _____

We stayed in (space, cabin # etc): _____

Most relaxing day: _____

_____

Something funny: _____

_____

Someone we met: _____

_____

Best story told: _____

_____

The kids liked this: _____

_____

The best food: _____

_____

Games played: _____

_____

Something disappointing: _____

_____

Next time I'll do this differently: _____

_____

Historic SAM Shortline Railroad
City: Cordele County: Crisp

Plan your trip: http://www.samshortline.com/

Activities:

- ❏ Bike Trails ❏
- ❏ Bird Watching ❏
- ❏ Boating ❏
- ❏ Fishing ❏
- ❏ Hiking ❏
- ❏ Historic Site ❏
- ❏ Hunting ❏
- ❏ Geocaching ❏
- ❏ Nature Trails ❏
- ❏ Watersports ❏
- ❏ Wildlife Viewing ❏

Facilities:

- ❏ ADA ❏
- ❏ Gift Shop ❏
- ❏ Museum ❏
- ❏ Visitor Center ❏
- ❏ Picnic sites ❏
- ❏ Restrooms ❏

Things to do in the area:

Get the Facts

- ❏ Phone 877-427-2457
- ❏ Park Hours _____
- ❏ Reservations? ____Y ____N
  date made_____
- ❏ Open all year? ____Y ____N
  dates_____
- ❏ Dog friendly ____Y ____N
- ❏ Distance from home
  miles: _____
  hours: _____
- ❏ Address_____
  _____
  _____

Fees:

- ❏ Day Use $ _____
- ❏ Refund policy
  _____
  _____
  _____

Notes:

Jefferson Davis Memorial State Historic Site
City: Fitzgerald   County: Irwin

Plan your trip: https://gastateparks.org/JeffersonDavisMemorial

Activities:

- ❑ Bike Trails   ❑
- ❑ Bird Watching   ❑
- ❑ Boating   ❑
- ❑ Fishing   ❑
- ❑ Hiking   ❑
- ❑ Historic Site   ❑
- ❑ Hunting   ❑
- ❑ Geocaching   ❑
- ❑ Nature Trails   ❑
- ❑ Watersports   ❑
- ❑ Wildlife Viewing   ❑

Facilities:

- ❑ ADA   ❑
- ❑ Gift Shop   ❑
- ❑ Museum   ❑
- ❑ Visitor Center   ❑
- ❑ Picnic sites   ❑
- ❑ Restrooms   ❑

Things to do in the area:

Get the Facts

- ❑ Phone 229-831-2335
- ❑ Park Hours _____
- ❑ Reservations? ____Y ____N
  date made_____
- ❑ Open all year? ____Y ____N
  dates_____
- ❑ Dog friendly ____Y ____N
- ❑ Distance from home
  miles: _____
  hours: _____
- ❑ Address_____
  _____
  _____

Fees:

- ❑ Day Use $ _____
- ❑ Refund policy
  _____
  _____
  _____

Notes:

Lapham-Patterson House State Historic Site

City: Thomasville   County: Thomas

Plan your trip: https://gastateparks.org/LaphamPattersonHouse

Activities:

- ❑ Bike Trails   ❑
- ❑ Bird Watching   ❑
- ❑ Boating   ❑
- ❑ Fishing   ❑
- ❑ Hiking   ❑
- ❑ Historic Site   ❑
- ❑ Hunting   ❑
- ❑ Geocaching   ❑
- ❑ Nature Trails   ❑
- ❑ Watersports   ❑
- ❑ Wildlife Viewing ❑

Facilities:

- ❑ ADA   ❑
- ❑ Gift Shop   ❑
- ❑ Museum   ❑
- ❑ Visitor Center   ❑
- ❑ Picnic sites   ❑
- ❑ Restrooms   ❑

Things to do in the area:

Get the Facts

- ❑ Phone 229-226-7664
- ❑ Park Hours _____
- ❑ Reservations? ____Y ____N
  date made_____
- ❑ Open all year? ____Y____N
  dates_____
- ❑ Dog friendly ____Y ____N
- ❑ Distance from home
  miles: _____
  hours: _____
- ❑ Address_____
  _____
  _____

Fees:

- ❑ Day Use $ _____
- ❑ Refund policy
  _____
  _____
  _____

Notes:

Ball's Ferry Property
City: Toomsboro   County: Wilkinson

Plan your trip: https://georgiawildlife.com/balls-ferry

Activities:

- ❑ Bike Trails ❑
- ❑ Bird Watching ❑
- ❑ Boating ❑
- ❑ Fishing ❑
- ❑ Hiking ❑
- ❑ Historic Site ❑
- ❑ Hunting ❑
- ❑ Geocaching ❑
- ❑ Nature Trails ❑
- ❑ Watersports ❑
- ❑ Wildlife Viewing ❑

Facilities:

- ❑ ADA ❑
- ❑ Gift Shop ❑
- ❑ Museum ❑
- ❑ Visitor Center ❑
- ❑ Picnic sites ❑
- ❑ Restrooms ❑

Things to do in the area:

Get the Facts

- ❑ Phone 706-595-4222
- ❑ Park Hours _____
- ❑ Reservations? ____Y ____N
  date made_____
- ❑ Open all year? ____Y____N
  dates_____
- ❑ Dog friendly ____Y ____N
- ❑ Distance from home
  miles: _____
  hours: _____
- ❑ Address_____
  _____
  _____

Fees:

- ❑ Day Use $ _____
- ❑ Refund policy
  _____
  _____
  _____

Notes:

Notes:

Laura S. Walker State Park

City: Waycross   **County: Brantley**

Plan your trip: https://gastateparks.org/LauraSWalker

Activities:

- ❑ Archery
- ❑ Biking Trails
- ❑ Boating
- ❑ Canoeing
- ❑ Canyon Climbing
- ❑ Caving
- ❑ Fishing
- ❑ Geocaching
- ❑ Hiking
- ❑ Historic Sites
- ❑ Horseback
- ❑ Hunting
- ❑ Kayaking
- ❑ Nature Programs
- ❑ Photography
- ❑ Rock Climbing
- ❑ Stargazing
- ❑ Swimming
- ❑ Water Skiing
- ❑ Wildlife & Bird Watching
- ❑ Ziplining

Facilities:

- ❑ ADA
- ❑ Picnic sites
- ❑ Restrooms
- ❑ Showers
- ❑ Trailer Access
- ❑ Visitor center
- ❑ Group Camping
- ❑ RV Camp
- ❑ Rustic Camping
- ❑ Cabins / Yurts
- ❑ Day Use Area

Notes:

Get the Facts

- ❑ Phone   912-287-4900
- ❑ Park Hours _____
- ❑ Reservations? ____Y ____N date made_____
- ❑ Open all year ____Y ____N dates_____
- ❑ Check in time _____
- ❑ Check out time _____
- ❑ Pet friendly ____Y ____N
- ❑ Max RV length _____
- ❑ Distance from home
  miles: _____
  hours: _____
- ❑ Address_____

Fees:

- ❑ Day Use $ _____
- ❑ Camp Sites $ _____
- ❑ RV Sites $ _____
- ❑ Refund policy _____

Make It Personal

Trip dates: _____ | The weather was: Sunny   Cloudy   Rainy   Stormy   Snowy   Foggy   Warm   Cold

Why I went:
_____

How I got there: (circle all that apply)   Plane   Train   Car   Bus   Bike   Hike   RV   MC

I went with:
_____

We stayed in (space, cabin # etc):
_____

Most relaxing day:
_____

Something funny:
_____

Someone we met:
_____

Best story told:
_____

The kids liked this:
_____

The best food:
_____

Games played:
_____

Something disappointing:
_____

Next time I'll do this differently:
_____

Fort McAllister State Park
City: Richmond Hill   County: Bryan
Plan your trip: https://gastateparks.org/FortMcAllister

Activities:

- ❏ Archery
- ❏ Biking Trails
- ❏ Boating
- ❏ Canoeing
- ❏ Canyon Climbing
- ❏ Caving
- ❏ Fishing
- ❏ Geocaching
- ❏ Hiking
- ❏ Historic Sites
- ❏ Horseback
- ❏ Hunting
- ❏ Kayaking
- ❏ Nature Programs
- ❏ Photography
- ❏ Rock Climbing
- ❏ Stargazing
- ❏ Swimming
- ❏ Water Skiing
- ❏ Wildlife & Bird Watching
- ❏ Ziplining

Facilities:

- ❏ ADA
- ❏ Picnic sites
- ❏ Restrooms
- ❏ Showers
- ❏ Trailer Access
- ❏ Visitor center
- ❏ Group Camping
- ❏ RV Camp
- ❏ Rustic Camping
- ❏ Cabins / Yurts
- ❏ Day Use Area

Notes:

Get the Facts

- ❏ Phone   912-727-2339
- ❏ Park Hours _____
- ❏ Reservations? ____Y ____N date made_____
- ❏ Open all year ____Y ____N dates_____
- ❏ Check in time _____
- ❏ Check out time _____
- ❏ Pet friendly ____Y ____N
- ❏ Max RV length _____
- ❏ Distance from home
  miles: _____
  hours: _____
- ❏ Address_____

Fees:

- ❏ Day Use $ _____
- ❏ Camp Sites $ _____
- ❏ RV Sites $ _____
- ❏ Refund policy _____

114

Make It Personal

Trip dates: _____ | The weather was: Sunny   Cloudy   Rainy   Stormy   Snowy   Foggy   Warm   Cold

Why I went:
_____

How I got there: (circle all that apply)   Plane   Train   Car   Bus   Bike   Hike   RV   MC

I went with:
_____

We stayed in (space, cabin # etc):
_____

Most relaxing day:
_____

Something funny:
_____

Someone we met:
_____

Best story told:
_____

The kids liked this:
_____

The best food:
_____

Games played:
_____

Something disappointing:
_____

Next time I'll do this differently:
_____
_____

Crooked River State Park
City: St. Marys County: Camden
Plan your trip: https://gastateparks.org/CrookedRiver

Activities:

- ☐ Archery
- ☐ Biking Trails
- ☐ Boating
- ☐ Canoeing
- ☐ Canyon Climbing
- ☐ Caving
- ☐ Fishing
- ☐ Geocaching
- ☐ Hiking
- ☐ Historic Sites
- ☐ Horseback
- ☐ Hunting
- ☐ Kayaking
- ☐ Nature Programs
- ☐ Photography
- ☐ Rock Climbing
- ☐ Stargazing
- ☐ Swimming
- ☐ Water Skiing
- ☐ Wildlife & Bird Watching
- ☐ Ziplining

Facilities:

- ☐ ADA
- ☐ Picnic sites
- ☐ Restrooms
- ☐ Showers
- ☐ Trailer Access
- ☐ Visitor center
- ☐ Group Camping
- ☐ RV Camp
- ☐ Rustic Camping
- ☐ Cabins / Yurts
- ☐ Day Use Area

Notes:

Get the Facts

- ☐ Phone   912-882-5256
- ☐ Park Hours _____
- ☐ Reservations? ____Y ____N date made_____
- ☐ Open all year ____Y ____N dates_____
- ☐ Check in time _____
- ☐ Check out time _____
- ☐ Pet friendly _____Y _____N
- ☐ Max RV length _____
- ☐ Distance from home
   miles: _____
   hours: _____
- ☐ Address_____

Fees:

- ☐ Day Use $ _____
- ☐ Camp Sites $ _____
- ☐ RV Sites $ _____
- ☐ Refund policy _____

Make It Personal

Trip dates: _____ | The weather was: Sunny   Cloudy   Rainy   Stormy   Snowy   Foggy   Warm   Cold

Why I went:
_____

How I got there: (circle all that apply)   Plane   Train   Car   Bus   Bike   Hike   RV   MC

I went with:
_____

We stayed in (space, cabin # etc):
_____

Most relaxing day:
_____

Something funny:
_____

Someone we met:
_____

Best story told:
_____

The kids liked this:
_____

The best food:
_____

Games played:
_____

Something disappointing:
_____

Next time I'll do this differently:
_____

Stephen C. Foster State Park

City: Fargo **County: Charlton**

Plan your trip: https://gastateparks.org/StephenCFoster

Activities:

- ❏ Archery
- ❏ Biking Trails
- ❏ Boating
- ❏ Canoeing
- ❏ Canyon Climbing
- ❏ Caving
- ❏ Fishing
- ❏ Geocaching
- ❏ Hiking
- ❏ Historic Sites
- ❏ Horseback
- ❏ Hunting
- ❏ Kayaking
- ❏ Nature Programs
- ❏ Photography
- ❏ Rock Climbing
- ❏ Stargazing
- ❏ Swimming
- ❏ Water Skiing
- ❏ Wildlife & Bird Watching
- ❏ Ziplining

Facilities:

- ❏ ADA
- ❏ Picnic sites
- ❏ Restrooms
- ❏ Showers
- ❏ Trailer Access
- ❏ Visitor center
- ❏ Group Camping
- ❏ RV Camp
- ❏ Rustic Camping
- ❏ Cabins / Yurts
- ❏ Day Use Area

Notes:

Get the Facts

- ❏ Phone   912-637-5274
- ❏ Park Hours _____
- ❏ Reservations? ____Y ____N date made_____
- ❏ Open all year ____Y ____N dates_____
- ❏ Check in time _____
- ❏ Check out time _____
- ❏ Pet friendly ____Y ____N
- ❏ Max RV length _____
- ❏ Distance from home
  miles: _____
  hours: _____
- ❏ Address_____

Fees:

- ❏ Day Use $ _____
- ❏ Camp Sites $ _____
- ❏ RV Sites $ _____
- ❏ Refund policy _____

Make It Personal

Trip dates: _____ | The weather was: Sunny Cloudy Rainy Stormy Snowy Foggy Warm Cold

Why I went: _____

_____

How I got there: (circle all that apply)   Plane   Train   Car   Bus   Bike   Hike   RV   MC

I went with: _____

We stayed in (space, cabin # etc): _____

Most relaxing day: _____

_____

Something funny: _____

_____

Someone we met: _____

_____

Best story told: _____

_____

The kids liked this: _____

_____

The best food: _____

_____

Games played: _____

_____

Something disappointing: _____

_____

Next time I'll do this differently: _____

_____

Skidaway Island State Park
City: Savannah   County: Chatham

Plan your trip: https://gastateparks.org/SkidawayIsland

Activities:

- ❑ Archery
- ❑ Biking Trails
- ❑ Boating
- ❑ Canoeing
- ❑ Canyon Climbing
- ❑ Caving
- ❑ Fishing
- ❑ Geocaching
- ❑ Hiking
- ❑ Historic Sites
- ❑ Horseback
- ❑ Hunting
- ❑ Kayaking
- ❑ Nature Programs
- ❑ Photography
- ❑ Rock Climbing
- ❑ Stargazing
- ❑ Swimming
- ❑ Water Skiing
- ❑ Wildlife & Bird Watching
- ❑ Ziplining

Facilities:

- ❑ ADA
- ❑ Picnic sites
- ❑ Restrooms
- ❑ Showers
- ❑ Trailer Access
- ❑ Visitor center
- ❑ Group Camping
- ❑ RV Camp
- ❑ Rustic Camping
- ❑ Cabins / Yurts
- ❑ Day Use Area

Notes:

Get the Facts

- ❑ Phone   912-598-2300
- ❑ Park Hours _____
- ❑ Reservations? ____Y ____N date made_____
- ❑ Open all year ____Y ____N dates_____
- ❑ Check in time _____
- ❑ Check out time _____
- ❑ Pet friendly _____Y _____N
- ❑ Max RV length _____
- ❑ Distance from home
  miles: _____
  hours: _____
- ❑ Address_____

Fees:

- ❑ Day Use $ _____
- ❑ Camp Sites $ _____
- ❑ RV Sites $ _____
- ❑ Refund policy _____

Make It Personal

Trip dates: _____ | The weather was: Sunny   Cloudy   Rainy   Stormy   Snowy   Foggy   Warm   Cold

Why I went:
_____
_____

How I got there: (circle all that apply)   Plane   Train   Car   Bus   Bike   Hike   RV   MC

I went with:
_____

We stayed in (space, cabin # etc):
_____

Most relaxing day:
_____
_____

Something funny:
_____
_____

Someone we met:
_____
_____

Best story told:
_____
_____

The kids liked this:
_____
_____

The best food:
_____
_____

Games played:
_____
_____

Something disappointing:
_____
_____

Next time I'll do this differently:
_____
_____

Georgia State Railroad Museum
City: Savannah   County: Chatham

Plan your trip: https://www.chsgeorgia.org/GSRM

Activities:

- ❑ Bike Trails ❑
- ❑ Bird Watching ❑
- ❑ Boating ❑
- ❑ Fishing ❑
- ❑ Hiking ❑
- ❑ Historic Site ❑
- ❑ Hunting ❑
- ❑ Geocaching ❑
- ❑ Nature Trails ❑
- ❑ Watersports ❑
- ❑ Wildlife Viewing ❑

Facilities:

- ❑ ADA ❑
- ❑ Gift Shop ❑
- ❑ Museum ❑
- ❑ Visitor Center ❑
- ❑ Picnic sites ❑
- ❑ Restrooms ❑

Things to do in the area:

Get the Facts

- ❑ Phone 912-651-6823
- ❑ Park Hours _____
- ❑ Reservations? ____Y ____N date made_____
- ❑ Open all year? ____Y ____N dates_____
- ❑ Dog friendly ____Y ____N
- ❑ Distance from home
  miles: _____
  hours: _____
- ❑ Address_____

Fees:

- ❑ Day Use $ _____
- ❑ Refund policy _____

Notes:

Harper Fowlkes House
City: Savannah   **County: Chatham**

Plan your trip: https://www.chsgeorgia.org/HFH

Activities:

- ❑ Bike Trails ❑
- ❑ Bird Watching ❑
- ❑ Boating ❑
- ❑ Fishing ❑
- ❑ Hiking ❑
- ❑ Historic Site ❑
- ❑ Hunting ❑
- ❑ Geocaching ❑
- ❑ Nature Trails ❑
- ❑ Watersports ❑
- ❑ Wildlife Viewing ❑

Facilities:

- ❑ ADA ❑
- ❑ Gift Shop ❑
- ❑ Museum ❑
- ❑ Visitor Center ❑
- ❑ Picnic sites ❑
- ❑ Restrooms ❑

Things to do in the area:

Get the Facts

- ❑ Phone 912-234-2180
- ❑ Park Hours _____
- ❑ Reservations? ____Y ____N
  date made _____
- ❑ Open all year? ____Y ____N
  dates _____
- ❑ Dog friendly ____Y ____N
- ❑ Distance from home
  miles: _____
  hours: _____
- ❑ Address _____
  _____
  _____

Fees:

- ❑ Day Use $ _____
- ❑ Refund policy
  _____
  _____
  _____

Notes:

Old Fort Jackson
City: Savannah   County: Chatham
Plan your trip: https://www.chsgeorgia.org/OFJ

Activities:

- ❑ Bike Trails ❑
- ❑ Bird Watching ❑
- ❑ Boating ❑
- ❑ Fishing ❑
- ❑ Hiking ❑
- ❑ Historic Site ❑
- ❑ Hunting ❑
- ❑ Geocaching ❑
- ❑ Nature Trails ❑
- ❑ Watersports ❑
- ❑ Wildlife Viewing ❑

Facilities:

- ❑ ADA ❑
- ❑ Gift Shop ❑
- ❑ Museum ❑
- ❑ Visitor Center ❑
- ❑ Picnic sites ❑
- ❑ Restrooms ❑

Things to do in the area:

Get the Facts

- ❑ Phone 912-232-3945
- ❑ Park Hours _____
- ❑ Reservations? ____Y ____N date made_____
- ❑ Open all year? ____Y____N dates_____
- ❑ Dog friendly ____Y ____N
- ❑ Distance from home miles: _____ hours: _____
- ❑ Address_____

Fees:

- ❑ Day Use $ _____
- ❑ Refund policy _____ _____ _____

Notes:

124

Pin Point Heritage Museum
City: Savannah   County: Chatham

Plan your trip: https://www.chsgeorgia.org/PHM

Activities:

- ❑ Bike Trails ❑
- ❑ Bird Watching ❑
- ❑ Boating ❑
- ❑ Fishing ❑
- ❑ Hiking ❑
- ❑ Historic Site ❑
- ❑ Hunting ❑
- ❑ Geocaching ❑
- ❑ Nature Trails ❑
- ❑ Watersports ❑
- ❑ Wildlife Viewing ❑

Facilities:

- ❑ ADA ❑
- ❑ Gift Shop ❑
- ❑ Museum ❑
- ❑ Visitor Center ❑
- ❑ Picnic sites ❑
- ❑ Restrooms ❑

Things to do in the area:

Get the Facts

- ❑ Phone 912-355-0064
- ❑ Park Hours _____
- ❑ Reservations? ____Y ____N date made_____
- ❑ Open all year? ____Y____N dates_____
- ❑ Dog friendly _____Y _____N
- ❑ Distance from home miles:_____ hours:_____
- ❑ Address_____ _____ _____

Fees:

- ❑ Day Use $ _____
- ❑ Refund policy _____ _____ _____

Notes:

Savannah History Museum

City: Savannah   **County: Chatham**

Plan your trip: https://www.chsgeorgia.org/SHM

Activities:

- ❏ Bike Trails ❏
- ❏ Bird Watching ❏
- ❏ Boating ❏
- ❏ Fishing ❏
- ❏ Hiking ❏
- ❏ Historic Site ❏
- ❏ Hunting ❏
- ❏ Geocaching ❏
- ❏ Nature Trails ❏
- ❏ Watersports ❏
- ❏ Wildlife Viewing ❏

Facilities:

- ❏ ADA ❏
- ❏ Gift Shop ❏
- ❏ Museum ❏
- ❏ Visitor Center ❏
- ❏ Picnic sites ❏
- ❏ Restrooms ❏

Things to do in the area:

Get the Facts

- ❏ Phone 912-651-6825
- ❏ Park Hours _____
- ❏ Reservations? ____Y ____N date made_____
- ❏ Open all year? ____Y ____N dates_____
- ❏ Dog friendly ____Y ____N
- ❏ Distance from home miles: _____ hours: _____
- ❏ Address_____

Fees:

- ❏ Day Use $ _____
- ❏ Refund policy _____

Notes:

Wormsloe State Historic Site
City: Savannah   County: Chatham

Plan your trip: https://gastateparks.org/Wormsloe

Activities:

- ❑ Bike Trails
- ❑ Bird Watching
- ❑ Boating
- ❑ Fishing
- ❑ Hiking
- ❑ Historic Site
- ❑ Hunting
- ❑ Geocaching
- ❑ Nature Trails
- ❑ Watersports
- ❑ Wildlife Viewing

Facilities:

- ❑ ADA
- ❑ Gift Shop
- ❑ Museum
- ❑ Visitor Center
- ❑ Picnic sites
- ❑ Restrooms

Things to do in the area:

Get the Facts

- ❑ Phone 912-353-3023
- ❑ Park Hours _____
- ❑ Reservations? ____Y ____N date made_____
- ❑ Open all year? ____Y ____N dates_____
- ❑ Dog friendly ____Y ____N
- ❑ Distance from home
  miles: _____
  hours: _____
- ❑ Address_____

Fees:

- ❑ Day Use $ _____
- ❑ Refund policy _____

Notes:

Hofwyl-Broadfield Plantation State Historic Site

City: Brunswick   **County: Glynn**

Plan your trip: https://gastateparks.org/HofwylBroadfieldPlantation

Activities:

- ❑ Bike Trails ❑
- ❑ Bird Watching ❑
- ❑ Boating ❑
- ❑ Fishing ❑
- ❑ Hiking ❑
- ❑ Historic Site ❑
- ❑ Hunting ❑
- ❑ Geocaching ❑
- ❑ Nature Trails ❑
- ❑ Watersports ❑
- ❑ Wildlife Viewing ❑

Facilities:

- ❑ ADA ❑
- ❑ Gift Shop ❑
- ❑ Museum ❑
- ❑ Visitor Center ❑
- ❑ Picnic sites ❑
- ❑ Restrooms ❑

Things to do in the area:

Get the Facts

- ❑ Phone 912-264-7333
- ❑ Park Hours _____
- ❑ Reservations? ____Y ____N date made_____
- ❑ Open all year? ____Y ____N dates_____
- ❑ Dog friendly ____Y ____N
- ❑ Distance from home
  miles: _____
  hours: _____
- ❑ Address_____

Fees:

- ❑ Day Use $ _____
- ❑ Refund policy _____

Notes:

Fort Morris State Historic Site
City: Midway   County: Liberty

Plan your trip: https://gastateparks.org/FortMorris

Activities:

- ❑ Bike Trails ❑
- ❑ Bird Watching ❑
- ❑ Boating ❑
- ❑ Fishing ❑
- ❑ Hiking ❑
- ❑ Historic Site ❑
- ❑ Hunting ❑
- ❑ Geocaching ❑
- ❑ Nature Trails ❑
- ❑ Watersports ❑
- ❑ Wildlife Viewing ❑

Facilities:

- ❑ ADA ❑
- ❑ Gift Shop ❑
- ❑ Museum ❑
- ❑ Visitor Center ❑
- ❑ Picnic sites ❑
- ❑ Restrooms ❑

Things to do in the area:

Get the Facts

- ❑ Phone 912-884-5999
- ❑ Park Hours _____
- ❑ Reservations? ____Y ____N
  date made_____
- ❑ Open all year? ____Y ____N
  dates_____
- ❑ Dog friendly ____Y ____N
- ❑ Distance from home
  miles: _____
  hours: _____
- ❑ Address_____
  _____
  _____

Fees:

- ❑ Day Use $ _____
- ❑ Refund policy
  _____
  _____
  _____

Notes:

Fort King George State Historic Site
City: Darien **County: McIntosh**

Plan your trip: https://gastateparks.org/FortKingGeorge

Activities:

- ❑ Bike Trails
- ❑ Bird Watching
- ❑ Boating
- ❑ Fishing
- ❑ Hiking
- ❑ Historic Site
- ❑ Hunting
- ❑ Geocaching
- ❑ Nature Trails
- ❑ Watersports
- ❑ Wildlife Viewing

Facilities:

- ❑ ADA
- ❑ Gift Shop
- ❑ Museum
- ❑ Visitor Center
- ❑ Picnic sites
- ❑ Restrooms

Things to do in the area:

Get the Facts

- ❑ Phone 912-437-4770
- ❑ Park Hours _____
- ❑ Reservations? ____Y ____N date made_____
- ❑ Open all year? ____Y ____N dates_____
- ❑ Dog friendly ____Y ____N
- ❑ Distance from home miles: _____ hours: _____
- ❑ Address _____

Fees:

- ❑ Day Use $ _____
- ❑ Refund policy _____

Notes:

Reynolds Mansion on Sapelo Island

City: Darien   **County: McIntosh**

Plan your trip: https://gastateparks.org/ReynoldsMansion

Activities:

- ❏ Bike Trails ❏
- ❏ Bird Watching ❏
- ❏ Boating ❏
- ❏ Fishing ❏
- ❏ Hiking ❏
- ❏ Historic Site ❏
- ❏ Hunting ❏
- ❏ Geocaching ❏
- ❏ Nature Trails ❏
- ❏ Watersports ❏
- ❏ Wildlife Viewing ❏

Facilities:

- ❏ ADA ❏
- ❏ Gift Shop ❏
- ❏ Museum ❏
- ❏ Visitor Center ❏
- ❏ Picnic sites ❏
- ❏ Restrooms ❏

Things to do in the area:

Get the Facts

- ❏ Phone 912-437-3224
- ❏ Park Hours _____
- ❏ Reservations? ____Y ____N
  date made _____
- ❏ Open all year? ____Y ____N
  dates _____
- ❏ Dog friendly ____Y ____N
- ❏ Distance from home
  miles: _____
  hours: _____
- ❏ Address _____
  _____
  _____

Fees:

- ❏ Day Use $ _____
- ❏ Refund policy
  _____
  _____
  _____

Notes:

Name:
City: County:
Plan your trip:

Activities:

- ☐ Archery
- ☐ Biking Trails
- ☐ Boating
- ☐ Canoeing
- ☐ Canyon Climbing
- ☐ Caving
- ☐ Fishing
- ☐ Geocaching
- ☐ Hiking
- ☐ Historic Sites
- ☐ Horseback
- ☐ Hunting
- ☐ Kayaking
- ☐ Nature Programs
- ☐ Photography
- ☐ Rock Climbing
- ☐ Stargazing
- ☐ Swimming
- ☐ Water Skiing
- ☐ Wildlife & Bird Watching
- ☐ Ziplining
- ☐
- ☐
- ☐
- ☐
- ☐
- ☐
- ☐
- ☐
- ☐

Facilities:

- ☐ ADA
- ☐ Picnic sites
- ☐ Restrooms
- ☐ Showers
- ☐ Trailer Access
- ☐ Visitor center
- ☐ Group Camping
- ☐ RV Camp
- ☐ Rustic Camping
- ☐ Cabins / Yurts
- ☐ Day Use Area

Notes:

Get the Facts

- ☐ Phone_____
- ☐ Park Hours _____
  _____
- ☐ Reservations? ____Y ____N
  date made_____
- ☐ Open all year ____Y ____N
  dates_____
- ☐ Check in time _____
- ☐ Check out time _____
- ☐ Pet friendly _____Y _____N
- ☐ Max RV length _____
- ☐ Distance from home
  miles: _____
  hours: _____
- ☐ Address_____
  _____
  _____

Fees:

- ☐ Day Use $ _____
- ☐ Camp Sites $ _____
- ☐ RV Sites $ _____
- ☐ Refund policy
  _____
  _____
  _____

Make It Personal

Trip dates: _____ | The weather was: Sunny Cloudy Rainy Stormy Snowy Foggy Warm Cold

Why I went:
_____

_____

How I got there: (circle all that apply)   Plane   Train   Car   Bus   Bike   Hike   RV   MC
_____

I went with:
_____

We stayed in (space, cabin # etc):
_____

Most relaxing day:
_____

_____

Something funny:
_____

_____

Someone we met:
_____

_____

Best story told:
_____

_____

The kids liked this:
_____

_____

The best food:
_____

_____

Games played:
_____

_____

Something disappointing:
_____

_____

Next time I'll do this differently:
_____

_____

Name:

City: County:
Plan your trip:

Activities:

- ❏ Archery
- ❏ Biking Trails
- ❏ Boating
- ❏ Canoeing
- ❏ Canyon Climbing
- ❏ Caving
- ❏ Fishing
- ❏ Geocaching
- ❏ Hiking
- ❏ Historic Sites
- ❏ Horseback
- ❏ Hunting
- ❏ Kayaking
- ❏ Nature Programs
- ❏ Photography
- ❏ Rock Climbing
- ❏ Stargazing
- ❏ Swimming
- ❏ Water Skiing
- ❏ Wildlife & Bird Watching
- ❏ Ziplining
- ❏
- ❏
- ❏
- ❏
- ❏
- ❏
- ❏
- ❏
- ❏

Facilities:

- ❏ ADA
- ❏ Picnic sites
- ❏ Restrooms
- ❏ Showers
- ❏ Trailer Access
- ❏ Visitor center
- ❏ Group Camping
- ❏ RV Camp
- ❏ Rustic Camping
- ❏ Cabins / Yurts
- ❏ Day Use Area

Notes:

Get the Facts

- ❏ Phone_____
- ❏ Park Hours _____
- ❏ Reservations? ____Y ____N
  date made_____
- ❏ Open all year ____Y ____N
  dates_____
- ❏ Check in time _____
- ❏ Check out time _____
- ❏ Pet friendly ____Y ____N
- ❏ Max RV length _____
- ❏ Distance from home
  miles: _____
  hours: _____
- ❏ Address_____
  _____
  _____

Fees:

- ❏ Day Use $ _____
- ❏ Camp Sites $ _____
- ❏ RV Sites $ _____
- ❏ Refund policy
  _____
  _____
  _____

Make It Personal

Trip dates: _____ | The weather was: Sunny Cloudy Rainy Stormy Snowy Foggy Warm Cold

Why I went:
_____
_____

How I got there: (circle all that apply)   Plane   Train   Car   Bus   Bike   Hike   RV   MC
_____

I went with:
_____

We stayed in (space, cabin # etc):
_____

Most relaxing day:
_____
_____

Something funny:
_____
_____

Someone we met:
_____
_____

Best story told:
_____
_____

The kids liked this:
_____
_____

The best food:
_____
_____

Games played:
_____
_____

Something disappointing:
_____
_____

Next time I'll do this differently:
_____
_____

Name:

City: **County:**

Plan your trip:

Activities:

- ❑ Archery
- ❑ Biking Trails
- ❑ Boating
- ❑ Canoeing
- ❑ Canyon Climbing
- ❑ Caving
- ❑ Fishing
- ❑ Geocaching
- ❑ Hiking
- ❑ Historic Sites
- ❑ Horseback
- ❑ Hunting
- ❑ Kayaking
- ❑ Nature Programs
- ❑ Photography
- ❑ Rock Climbing
- ❑ Stargazing
- ❑ Swimming
- ❑ Water Skiing
- ❑ Wildlife & Bird Watching
- ❑ Ziplining
- ❑ _____
- ❑ _____
- ❑ _____
- ❑ _____
- ❑ _____
- ❑ _____
- ❑ _____
- ❑ _____
- ❑ _____
- ❑ _____

Facilities:

- ❑ ADA
- ❑ Picnic sites
- ❑ Restrooms
- ❑ Showers
- ❑ Trailer Access
- ❑ Visitor center
- ❑ Group Camping
- ❑ RV Camp
- ❑ Rustic Camping
- ❑ Cabins / Yurts
- ❑ Day Use Area

Notes:

Get the Facts

- ❑ Phone_____
- ❑ Park Hours
  _____
- ❑ Reservations? ____Y ____N
  date made_____
- ❑ Open all year ____Y ____N
  dates_____
- ❑ Check in time _____
- ❑ Check out time _____
- ❑ Pet friendly _____Y _____N
- ❑ Max RV length _____
- ❑ Distance from home
  miles: _____
  hours: _____
- ❑ Address_____
  _____
  _____

Fees:

- ❑ Day Use $ _____
- ❑ Camp Sites $ _____
- ❑ RV Sites $ _____
- ❑ Refund policy
  _____
  _____
  _____

Make It Personal

Trip dates: _____ | The weather was: Sunny   Cloudy   Rainy   Stormy   Snowy   Foggy   Warm   Cold

Why I went:
_____

_____

How I got there: (circle all that apply)   Plane   Train   Car   Bus   Bike   Hike   RV   MC
_____

I went with:
_____

We stayed in (space, cabin # etc):
_____

Most relaxing day:
_____

_____

Something funny:
_____

_____

Someone we met:
_____

_____

Best story told:
_____

_____

The kids liked this:
_____

_____

The best food:
_____

_____

Games played:
_____

_____

Something disappointing:
_____

_____

Next time I'll do this differently:
_____

_____

Name:

City: **County:**

Plan your trip:

Activities:

- ❑ Archery
- ❑ Biking Trails
- ❑ Boating
- ❑ Canoeing
- ❑ Canyon Climbing
- ❑ Caving
- ❑ Fishing
- ❑ Geocaching
- ❑ Hiking
- ❑ Historic Sites
- ❑ Horseback
- ❑ Hunting
- ❑ Kayaking
- ❑ Nature Programs
- ❑ Photography
- ❑ Rock Climbing
- ❑ Stargazing
- ❑ Swimming
- ❑ Water Skiing
- ❑ Wildlife & Bird Watching
- ❑ Ziplining

Facilities:

- ❑ ADA
- ❑ Picnic sites
- ❑ Restrooms
- ❑ Showers
- ❑ Trailer Access
- ❑ Visitor center
- ❑ Group Camping
- ❑ RV Camp
- ❑ Rustic Camping
- ❑ Cabins / Yurts
- ❑ Day Use Area

Notes:

Get the Facts

- ❑ Phone_____
- ❑ Park Hours _____
- ❑ Reservations? ____Y ____N date made_____
- ❑ Open all year ____Y ____N dates_____
- ❑ Check in time _____
- ❑ Check out time _____
- ❑ Pet friendly _____Y _____N
- ❑ Max RV length _____
- ❑ Distance from home
  miles: _____
  hours: _____
- ❑ Address_____
  _____
  _____

Fees:

- ❑ Day Use $ _____
- ❑ Camp Sites $ _____
- ❑ RV Sites $ _____
- ❑ Refund policy _____
  _____
  _____

Make It Personal

Trip dates: _____ | The weather was: Sunny Cloudy Rainy Stormy Snowy Foggy Warm Cold

Why I went:
_____

_____

How I got there: (circle all that apply)   Plane   Train   Car   Bus   Bike   Hike   RV   MC
_____

I went with:
_____

We stayed in (space, cabin # etc):
_____

Most relaxing day:
_____

_____

Something funny:
_____

_____

Someone we met:
_____

_____

Best story told:
_____

_____

The kids liked this:
_____

_____

The best food:
_____

_____

Games played:
_____

_____

Something disappointing:
_____

_____

Next time I'll do this differently:
_____

_____

Name:
City: **County:**

Plan your trip:

Activities:

- ❑ Archery
- ❑ Biking Trails
- ❑ Boating
- ❑ Canoeing
- ❑ Canyon Climbing
- ❑ Caving
- ❑ Fishing
- ❑ Geocaching
- ❑ Hiking
- ❑ Historic Sites
- ❑ Horseback
- ❑ Hunting
- ❑ Kayaking
- ❑ Nature Programs
- ❑ Photography
- ❑ Rock Climbing
- ❑ Stargazing
- ❑ Swimming
- ❑ Water Skiing
- ❑ Wildlife & Bird Watching
- ❑ Ziplining
- ❑
- ❑
- ❑
- ❑
- ❑
- ❑
- ❑
- ❑
- ❑
- ❑

Facilities:

- ❑ ADA
- ❑ Picnic sites
- ❑ Restrooms
- ❑ Showers
- ❑ Trailer Access
- ❑ Visitor center
- ❑ Group Camping
- ❑ RV Camp
- ❑ Rustic Camping
- ❑ Cabins / Yurts
- ❑ Day Use Area

Notes:

Get the Facts

- ❑ Phone_____
- ❑ Park Hours
  _____
- ❑ Reservations? ____Y ____N
  date made_____
- ❑ Open all year ____Y____N
  dates_____
- ❑ Check in time _____
- ❑ Check out time _____
- ❑ Pet friendly _____Y _____N
- ❑ Max RV length _____
- ❑ Distance from home
  miles: _____
  hours: _____
- ❑ Address_____
  _____
  _____

Fees:

- ❑ Day Use $ _____
- ❑ Camp Sites $ _____
- ❑ RV Sites $ _____
- ❑ Refund policy
  _____
  _____
  _____

Make It Personal

Trip dates: _____ | The weather was: Sunny   Cloudy   Rainy   Stormy   Snowy   Foggy   Warm   Cold

Why I went:
_____

How I got there: (circle all that apply)   Plane   Train   Car   Bus   Bike   Hike   RV   MC

I went with:
_____

We stayed in (space, cabin # etc):
_____

Most relaxing day:
_____

Something funny:
_____

Someone we met:
_____

Best story told:
_____

The kids liked this:
_____

The best food:
_____

Games played:
_____

Something disappointing:
_____

Next time I'll do this differently:
_____
_____

Name:
City: County:
Plan your trip:

Activities:

- ☐ Bike Trails ☐
- ☐ Bird Watching ☐
- ☐ Boating ☐
- ☐ Fishing ☐
- ☐ Hiking ☐
- ☐ Historic Site ☐
- ☐ Hunting ☐
- ☐ Geocaching ☐
- ☐ Nature Trails ☐
- ☐ Watersports ☐
- ☐ Wildlife Viewing ☐

Facilities:

- ☐ ADA ☐
- ☐ Gift Shop ☐
- ☐ Museum ☐
- ☐ Visitor Center ☐
- ☐ Picnic sites ☐
- ☐ Restrooms ☐

Things to do in the area:

Get the Facts

- ☐ Phone_____
- ☐ Park Hours
  _____
- ☐ Reservations? ____Y ____N
  date made_____
- ☐ Open all year? ____Y____N
  dates_____
- ☐ Dog friendly _____Y _____N
- ☐ Distance from home
  miles: _____
  hours: _____
- ☐ Address_____
  _____
  _____

Fees:

- ☐ Day Use $ _____
- ☐ Refund policy
  _____
  _____
  _____

Notes:

142

Name:
City: County:
Plan your trip:

Activities:

- ☐ Bike Trails ☐
- ☐ Bird Watching ☐
- ☐ Boating ☐
- ☐ Fishing ☐
- ☐ Hiking ☐
- ☐ Historic Site ☐
- ☐ Hunting ☐
- ☐ Geocaching ☐
- ☐ Nature Trails ☐
- ☐ Watersports ☐
- ☐ Wildlife Viewing ☐

Facilities:

- ☐ ADA ☐
- ☐ Gift Shop ☐
- ☐ Museum ☐
- ☐ Visitor Center ☐
- ☐ Picnic sites ☐
- ☐ Restrooms ☐

Things to do in the area:

Get the Facts

- ☐ Phone _____
- ☐ Park Hours _____
- ☐ Reservations? ____Y ____N date made _____
- ☐ Open all year? ____Y ____N dates _____
- ☐ Dog friendly ____Y ____N
- ☐ Distance from home miles: _____ hours: _____
- ☐ Address _____ _____ _____

Fees:

- ☐ Day Use $ _____
- ☐ Refund policy _____ _____ _____

Notes:

Name:
City: County:
Plan your trip:

Activities:

- ☐ Bike Trails ☐
- ☐ Bird Watching ☐
- ☐ Boating ☐
- ☐ Fishing ☐
- ☐ Hiking ☐
- ☐ Historic Site ☐
- ☐ Hunting ☐
- ☐ Geocaching ☐
- ☐ Nature Trails ☐
- ☐ Watersports ☐
- ☐ Wildlife Viewing ☐

Facilities:

- ☐ ADA ☐
- ☐ Gift Shop ☐
- ☐ Museum ☐
- ☐ Visitor Center ☐
- ☐ Picnic sites ☐
- ☐ Restrooms ☐

Things to do in the area:

Get the Facts

- ☐ Phone_____
- ☐ Park Hours
  _____
- ☐ Reservations? ____Y ____N
  date made_____
- ☐ Open all year? ____Y ____N
  dates_____
- ☐ Dog friendly _____Y _____N
- ☐ Distance from home
  miles: _____
  hours: _____
- ☐ Address_____
  _____
  _____

Fees:

- ☐ Day Use $ _____
- ☐ Refund policy
  _____
  _____
  _____

Notes:

Name:
City: ## County:
Plan your trip:

Activities:

- ❏ Bike Trails   ❏
- ❏ Bird Watching   ❏
- ❏ Boating   ❏
- ❏ Fishing   ❏
- ❏ Hiking   ❏
- ❏ Historic Site   ❏
- ❏ Hunting   ❏
- ❏ Geocaching   ❏
- ❏ Nature Trails   ❏
- ❏ Watersports   ❏
- ❏ Wildlife Viewing   ❏

Facilities:

- ❏ ADA   ❏
- ❏ Gift Shop   ❏
- ❏ Museum   ❏
- ❏ Visitor Center   ❏
- ❏ Picnic sites   ❏
- ❏ Restrooms   ❏

Things to do in the area:

Get the Facts

- ❏ Phone _____
- ❏ Park Hours
  _____
- ❏ Reservations? ____Y ____N
  date made_____
- ❏ Open all year? ____Y____N
  dates_____
- ❏ Dog friendly ____Y____N
- ❏ Distance from home
  miles: _____
  hours: _____
- ❏ Address_____
  _____
  _____

Fees:

- ❏ Day Use $ _____
- ❏ Refund policy
  _____
  _____
  _____

Notes:

145

Name:
City: ## County:
Plan your trip:

Activities:

- ☐ Bike Trails   ☐
- ☐ Bird Watching   ☐
- ☐ Boating   ☐
- ☐ Fishing   ☐
- ☐ Hiking   ☐
- ☐ Historic Site   ☐
- ☐ Hunting   ☐
- ☐ Geocaching   ☐
- ☐ Nature Trails   ☐
- ☐ Watersports   ☐
- ☐ Wildlife Viewing   ☐

Facilities:

- ☐ ADA   ☐
- ☐ Gift Shop   ☐
- ☐ Museum   ☐
- ☐ Visitor Center   ☐
- ☐ Picnic sites   ☐
- ☐ Restrooms   ☐

Things to do in the area:

Get the Facts

- ☐ Phone_____
- ☐ Park Hours
  _____
- ☐ Reservations? ____Y ____N
  date made_____
- ☐ Open all year? ____Y____N
  dates_____
- ☐ Dog friendly _____Y _____N
- ☐ Distance from home
  miles: _____
  hours: _____
- ☐ Address_____
  _____
  _____

Fees:

- ☐ Day Use $ _____
- ☐ Refund policy
  _____
  _____
  _____

Notes:

146

INDEX

- ❑ A.H. Stephens State Park..................74
- ❑ Amicalola Falls State Park & Lodge..........14
- ❑ Ball's Ferry Property..........................109
- ❑ Black Rock Mountain State Park.............22
- ❑ Chattahoochee Bend State Park.............46
- ❑ Chief Vann House State Historic Site........36
- ❑ Cloudland Canyon State Park................12
- ❑ Crooked River State Park....................116
- ❑ Dahlonega Gold Museum State HS..........35
- ❑ Don Carter State Park........................56
- ❑ Elijah Clark State Park........................64
- ❑ Etowah Indian Mounds State HS.............32
- ❑ F. D. Roosevelt State Park....................58
- ❑ Florence Marina State Park.................100
- ❑ Fort King George State Historic Site........130
- ❑ Fort McAllister State Park...................114
- ❑ Fort Morris State Historic Site...............129
- ❑ Fort Mountain State Park....................18
- ❑ Fort Yargo State Park.........................40
- ❑ General Coffee State Park....................84
- ❑ George L. Smith State Park..................92
- ❑ George T. Bagby State Park..................82
- ❑ Georgia State Railroad Museum............122
- ❑ Georgia Veterans State Park.................88
- ❑ Hamburg State Park..........................76
- ❑ Hard Labor Creek State Park................72
- ❑ Hardman Farm State Historic Site..........38
- ❑ Harper Fowlkes House......................123
- ❑ Hartwell Lakeside Park......................60
- ❑ High Falls State Park..........................70
- ❑ Historic SAM Shortline Railroad............106
- ❑ Hofwyl-Broadfield Plantation State Historic Site..128
- ❑ Indian Springs State Park....................42
- ❑ Jack Hill State Park..........................102
- ❑ James H. Floyd State Park....................10
- ❑ Jarrell Plantation State Historic Site..........78
- ❑ Jefferson Davis Memorial State HS..........107
- ❑ Kolomoki Mounds State Park.................90
- ❑ Lapham-Patterson House State HS.........108
- ❑ Laura S. Walker State Park..................112
- ❑ Little Ocmulgee State Park & Lodge........104
- ❑ Magnolia Springs State Park.................94
- ❑ Mistletoe State Park..........................44
- ❑ Moccasin Creek State Park..................20
- ❑ New Echota State Historic Site..............33
- ❑ Old Fort Jackson..............................124
- ❑ Panola Mountain State Park.................62
- ❑ Pickett's Mill Battlefield State Historic Site..37
- ❑ Pin Point Heritage Museum.................125
- ❑ Providence Canyon State Outdoor Recreation Area................................98
- ❑ Red Top Mountain State Park.................8
- ❑ Reed Bingham State Park....................86
- ❑ Resaca Battlefield.............................34
- ❑ Reynolds Mansion on Sapelo Island........131
- ❑ Richard B. Russell State Park................50
- ❑ Robert Toombs House State HS.............80
- ❑ Rocky Mountain Recreation & Public Fishing Area..16
- ❑ Roosevelt's Little White House State Historic Site..................................68
- ❑ Savannah History Museum.................126
- ❑ Seminole State Park..........................96
- ❑ Skidaway Island State Park.................120
- ❑ Smithgall Woods State Park..................28
- ❑ Stephen C. Foster State Park................118
- ❑ Sweetwater Creek State Park................48
- ❑ Tallulah Gorge State Park....................24
- ❑ Traveler's Rest State Historic Site...........79
- ❑ Tugaloo State Park............................52
- ❑ Unicoi State Park & Lodge...................30
- ❑ Victoria Bryant State Park....................54
- ❑ Vogel State Park..............................26
- ❑ Watson Mill Bridge State Park...............66
- ❑ Wormsloe State Historic Site...............127

Add More Overnight Parks
- ❑ _____132
- ❑ _____134
- ❑ _____136
- ❑ _____138
- ❑ _____140

Add More Day Use Parks
- ❑ _____142
- ❑ _____143
- ❑ _____144
- ❑ _____145
- ❑ _____146

Notes: